STREET TALK
Character Monologues
For Actors

GLENN ALTERMAN: As an actor, Glenn Alterman has appeared in regional theatres, off-Broadway, on all the New York soaps, and in several films; including, most recently, playing opposite Woody Allen and Bette Midler in Paul Mazursky's *Scenes from a Mall*. His plays include: *Kiss Me When It's Over*, commissioned by E. Weissman Productions (La Mama); *Heartstrings*, book for the musical, commissioned by the Design Industries Foundation For Aids, 30 city tour with a cast of 30 including Michelle Pfeiffer, Ron Silver, Christopher Reeve, Susan Sarandon, Marlo Thomas and Sandy Duncan; *Tourists of the Mindfield*, semi-finalist in the L. Arnold Weissberger Playwriting Competition at New Dramatists, New York; *Dirty Prayers*, commissioned by Sydelle Marshall; and *God in Bed*, premiered at the West Bank Café Downstairs Theater Bar. A new production, *Street Talk* (excerpts from the book) will premiere at the West Coast Ensemble this spring.

ANDRÉ DE SHIELDS has appeared in numerous Broadway productions and received an Emmy for his role in the NBC television special based on the musical *Ain't Misbehavin'*. He holds a degree in English from the University of Wisconsin and is currently a Master's candidate at NYU. De Shields is the Algur H. Meadows Distinguished Visiting Professor in the Meadows School of the Arts at Southern Methodist University in Dallas, Texas.

STREET TALK
Character Monologues
For Actors

Glenn Alterman

SK
A Smith and Kraus Book

A Smith and Kraus Book
Published by Smith and Kraus, Inc.

Cover design by David Wise
Text design by Jeannette Champagne

Manufactured on recycled paper in the United States of America

First Edition: May 1991
10 9 8 7 6 5 4 3 2 1

Publisher's Cataloging in Publication
(Prepared by Quality Books Inc.)

Alterman, Glenn, 1946-
  Street Talk: character monologues for actors / Glenn Alterman. --

  p. cm.
  ISBN 0-9622722-5-6

  1. Monologues. 2. Drama--Collections. 3. Acting. I. Title

PN2080   808.82
                                  91-60871

Smith and Kraus, Inc.
Main Street, P.O. Box 10, Newbury, Vermont 05051
(802) 866-5423

Quality Printing and binding by Eagle Printing Co., Inc., Albany, New York 12202, U.S.A

iv

ACKNOWLEDGMENTS

The playwright wishes to thank the following: Wynn Handman, Annamarie Kostura C.S.A., Ellen Stewart, Meryl Vladmir (La Mama), Terry Schreiber, André De Shields, Leslie (Hoban) Blake, Dan and Dee Weber, Sadie Rosenthal, Helen Harvey and Mimi Materras, Joe Sullivan, Kathryn Luster, Michael Howard, Greg Jackson, Paul Mazursky, Viv Bell, Blanche Chavoiste, John Dickson Fisher, Eva Charney, Sydelle Marshall, Spider Duncan Christopher, Bonnie and Sam Elmowitz, Patrick Calkins, Carlotta Schott, Gloria Slofkiss, Steve Olson, Rowen Joseph, Rand Forrester (the guys at the West Bank Café Downstairs Theater Bar) and all the producers, directors and actors who gave their time, energy and creativity.

CONTENTS

CONTENTS

CONTENTS

Section II - Monologues for Women

CONTENTS

FOREWORD

Have you ever been in Times Square on New Year's Eve, locked in a shoulder-to-shoulder crush of a quarter million diverse people? Well, if you've ever experienced that scene, you already know the kind of excitement to be found in Glenn Alterman's <u>Street Talk</u>.

Here are tortured souls who race through their lives with the terrifying speed of a rollercoaster. Here is the giant ferris wheel that takes people to breathless heights.

Made vivid by a rage of introspection, Alterman's people find God in bed or in a dirty prayer, or sitting on the steps of a church on Forty-Ninth Street. A lucky few discover God in themselves. The women and men you meet here live lives of tragic beauty and brutally plain truth, a truth that's best illuminated in the light of street lamps or glowing neon. Every story is a parable about people who have kissed, maybe danced with the Devil, and lived to tell about it.

There is here the potential for immense gratification for the actor who does not shrink away from the powerful exhilaration of exorcising emotional demons.

—André De Shields

INTRODUCTION

Like most actors, I have spent a lot of time searching for the perfect monologue. That search has taken me on a journey into writing.

Over the years, I have logged countless hours reading through thousands of plays in search of that one, elusive, perfect piece containing a character that would grab and move me.

Finally, feeling somewhat frustrated, I decided to write my own piece. I sat at my desk and began by doing funny little improvs by myself, letting my imagination go wild. Much to my delight, words, bits of dialogue and strange new ideas started popping right out of me! I jotted down everything I could; grabbing from the free flow of images, ideas and memories. I then started to put it all together. First, a character began to emerge. Then, a situation. I molded the two together, reworking them to form a piece and then: rewriting, rewriting, rewriting. A few days later, I had completed my first monologue: the story of Sal, a man who meets a Martian in his diner.

At the time I was studying acting with Wynn Handman. One night, I brought Sal to class and quickly learned that there's nothing more frightening than performing your own monologue for the first time in public. Fortunately, Sal was a hit. I was on to something.

I set to writing monologues in earnest. I was turning them out by the truckload. Some of them really flew. Others took nose dives. This process made me keenly aware of what other actors were looking for. I saw what worked, what didn't and why.

I eventually wound up with a great stack of effective pieces. It struck me that I had the makings of a play in my hands. I developed this idea, and a few months later, I had the first reading of *GOD IN BED*: a play about the folks on 42nd Street; their dreams, hopes, cravings and downfalls.

Producer-director Spider Duncan Christopher offered to mount a production of *GOD IN BED* at the West Bank Café Downstairs Theater Bar. I'd heard about the West Bank. It was

INTRODUCTION

becoming the Café Cino of the 80's: a place where actors, writers and directors could hone their crafts in a secure environment.

In March of 1988, *GOD IN BED* opened under the direction of Spider at the West Bank Café with a first rate cast. The next few years witnessed the West Bank premieres of *TOURISTS OF THE MINDFIELD* and *DIRTY PRAYERS*.

Since then, I have received continuing requests from auditioning actors, that I make my monologues available. Thus, Street Talk. Hopefully, you will find your perfect monologue is in these pages. In any event, I believe that this book will provide you with an abundance of worthy material from which to choose. Good luck!

—Glenn Alterman
New York City
February, 1991

PRODUCTION INFORMATION

GOD IN BED was first presented at the West Bank Café Downstairs Theater Bar, New York City, on March 21, 1988. It was produced by Spidercorp Productions. The director was Spider Duncan. It appeared with the following cast in order of appearance:

Sam	*Kevin Harrah*
Harris	*Leland Gantt*
Stella	*Cynthia Martells*
Ralph	*John Cygan*
Kathy	*Dian Ainslee*
Marcus	*Gordon Joseph Weiss*
Mary-Anne	*Dian Ainslee*
Prince	*Leland Gantt*
Lefty	*John Cygan*
Waitress	*Jennifer Williams*
John	*Gordon Joseph Weiss*
Mary	*Jennifer Williams*
Tommy	*John Cygan*
Rose	*Jennifer Williams*
Joe	*John Cygan*
Michael	*Gordon Joseph Weiss*
Jane	*Dian Ainslee*
José	*Gordon Joseph Weiss*

PRODUCTION INFORMATION

TOURISTS OF THE MINDFIELD was first presented at the West Bank Café Downstairs Theater Bar, New York City, on March 8, 1989. The producer was Gloria Productions. The director was Glenn Alterman. Casting director was Annamarie Kostura C.S.A. Lighting design was by Rand Forrester. The stage manager was Shelly Broughton. It appeared with the following cast in order of appearance:

Paulie	*Rob McCaskill*
The Wash	*Susan Aston*
The Big Pool	*Dan Grimaldi*
Ethan	*Gordon Joseph Weiss*
Rita	*Lynn Cohen*
Vince	*Dan Grimaldi*
Lila	*Susan Aston*
T.S.	*Gordon Joseph Weiss*
Sal	*John Cygan*
Marie	*Lynn Cohen*
Disappearance	*Rob McCaskill*
Shirl	*Lynn Cohen*
Home	*John Cygan*

PRODUCTION INFORMATION

TOURISTS OF THE MINDFIELD was performed at Playwrights Horizons (Second Stage), New York City, on March 20, 1989. Subsequently it re-opened at the West Bank Café Downstairs Theater Bar on June 5, 1989. The producer was Gloria Productions. The director was Glenn Alterman. Casting director was Annamarie Kostura, C.S.A. The stage manager was Shelly Broughton (later it was Carol Venezia). It appeared with the following cast in order of appearance:

Paulie	*Rob McCaskill*
The Wash	*Susan Aston*
The Big Pool	*Dan Grimaldi (later by Bob Ari)*
Mein Johnny in Germany	*Jennifer Williams*
Ethan	*Gordon Joseph Weiss*
Rita	*Mary Louise Burke*
Vince	*Dan Grimaldi (later by Bob Ari)*
Lila	*Susan Aston*
T.S.	*Gordon Joseph Weiss*
Hannah	*Susan Aston*
Sal	*John Cygan*
Marie	*Mary Louise Burke (later by Helen Hanft)*
Disappearance	*Rob McCaskill*
Lulu	*Mary Louise Burke*
Home	*John Cygan*
Sheila	*Helen Hanft*

PRODUCTION INFORMATION

KISS ME WHEN IT'S OVER was first produced at La Mama ETC, New York City, on January 4, 1990. The producer was Eric Weissman Productions. The director was André De Shields. Musical director was James Mironchik. Choreography was by Wayne Cilento. Scenic design by John DeFazio. Lighting by Howard Thies. Costume design by Chico Kasinoir. The stage manager was Rachel Levine. The producton assistant was Miguel Braganza II. It appeared with the following cast in order of appearance:

Sam	*Rob McCaskill*
Piano Man	*André De Shields*
The French Singer	*Jeffrey Herman*
Big A	*Nicholas Levitin*
Carousel	*Adrian Bailey*
Murray	*Rob McCaskill*
Velvet	*Susan Aston*
Angel	*Amy Coleman*
Henny	*Susan Aston*
Brian	*Nicholas Levitin*
Helen	*Helen Hanft*
Singers	*Gina Taylor*
	Frieda Williams

PRODUCTION INFORMATION

DIRTY PRAYERS was first produced at the West Bank Café Downstairs Theater Bar, New York City, on March 8, 1990. The producer was Sydelle Marshall. The director was Glenn Alterman. Casting director was Leslie (Hoban) Blake. Lighting design was by Patrick Eagleton. The stage manager was Paul A. Kochman. It appeared with the following cast in order of appearance:

Flora	*Yvette Edelhart*
Tony	*Nelson Avidon*
Anna	*Stephanie Berry*
Mr. Christianson	*John Bigham*
Sid Schwartz	*Harvey Siegel*
Beth	*Spring Condoyan*
Melvin Stein	*Larry Fleishman*
Angela	*Stephanie Berry*
Johnny Star	*Mathew Cowles*
Eva	*Regina Scott*

STREET TALK
Character Monologues
For Actors

HOME

Casey - 20's - A small prison cell
Casey, a soldier, has been captured by the enemy and locked in
a cramped prison cell. Time and loneliness have taken their toll
on him. He tries to explain to his Captain what life in the
prison cell has been like for him.

CASEY: ...And Casper...Casper talks to me. So does Daffy Duck,
Elmer Fudd, whoever. All of 'em. And we'll have a smoke, couple
of drinks, shoot the shit, whatever. An' per usual, Daffy or
Donald'll rag about the shit they've been going through with Walt
Disney and the studio brass. How cartoon folks get screwed by the
studio big wigs at Warner Brothers. And it's a shame. It is. I feel
for them. I do. I empathize. And so I'm listening deeply, when
this buzz goes through me, ya know? Some streak of sanity jolts me
for a second, making me think, "Hey! Wait! Stop! There's no one
here! Ya lost track. You're in Luna City, soldier; up in ya head."
And I realize, I'd forgotten where I was. And where that is Captain,
of course, is here. Right here where we're sitting. On this dirty
mattress on the floor, where I've been for I don't know how long.
By myself, in this two by four cell, without windows or light.
Locked up like some animal... And there are no cartoon people. I
know that. And then I realize I've been havin' the crazies. Gone
koo-koo from bein' here too long. A captive in this country, far
from anyone I know. Being held by a group of asshole terrorists,
whose fuckin' names I can't even pronounce. And these guys don't
have the balls to show me their faces. Or the courtesy, the human
kindness, to screw a fuckin' lightbulb in here; so I'm not always left
sitting in the pitch black—as I have been. Never knowing if it's
night or day. Or even if I'm awake or asleep. And it's the not
knowing sir, the not knowing that makes you crazy. Because it all
starts to blend. One gray night. And that's when the cartoon people
show up. It's then that my thoughts begin turning into these little
toys that I play with. You heard me. My thoughts, I can hold
them, sir. Play with them in my fingers like this. *(he does)* And

1

HOME

I start bouncing them off the walls, like little beach balls. Hundreds of them. Ping. Ping. Ping.

And eventually, what finally happens, Captain, is that this cell becomes filled with beach balls bouncing everywhere. Ping! Ping! Ping! And I can't move. I'm crowded out by my own thoughts. Isn't that odd? And when there's no room left, just before I'm ready to flip out from the claustraphobia, right before I scream, PING! PING! PING!—I snap out of it. And I remember where I am. And I feel some hope. Hopeful. And believe someone will be here soon. Someone from home, who'll rescue me. Someone from America who knows I'm alive. And it's that hope that's kept me sane, sir. And it's then that I remember, Captain, I've been trained. We are sir. Well trained, and prepared for this. And I realize my mind is stronger than this. I will not give up, go under. Never!

So in the middle of the beach balls bouncing, ping, ping, ping. And the cartoon people rallying for my attention in Luna Land, I pull it together, sir. Sing a song, say the pledge of allegiance, anything. Anything to grab on to in that moment of need; that'll bring be back home, to myself. Myself—home. Once again in charge. Strong and solid. Once again in reality. Good ole reality—waiting. Which gets me to now. This moment—here with you. Finally, finally rescued. And we're goin' back, right, sir? Back home? Back to the U.S. of A. We're goin'… *(he turns and whispers)* "Casper, Elmer come on guys. This is it. We made it. We're goin' back. Come on…" *(he turns around, smiles, then)* "Captain???… Where??… Captain!!?? Captain!!!"

2

THE BIG POOL

Herschel - Middle aged - Poolside at a resort
Herschel, a loud, sleazy, two-bit talent agent has just met a new
friend while having drinks around the pool. After they've gotten
to know each other, he shares his views on fame, women, and
the good life.

HERSCHEL: *(He is middle-aged, overweight, wearing bright floral
print boxer swim shorts. He is sitting in a chaise lounge by a
swimming pool, holding a Collins glass half filled with ice. Most of
the drink is gone. On a nearby table is an ashtray with a cigar
burning. He is loud, aggressive, and in the heat of conversation)*
Every club! Every dump! Name a room, from here to there, and
I played it. Vegas, Miami, Catskills. And I'm talking big money.
Big, big, money. These kids today—*pishas! (claps hands)* One-
two-three, there on Carson. Then quick as shit, they land a multi-
movie deal. S'too easy. Where's the working for it? *(takes an ice
cube from glass, hurls it to ground)* Where's the breaking your
back, huh?! And if you're black! *(angrily hurls another cube)* If
you're *black*, you got it made! It's easy street! Forget about it.
You tell a couple a dirty jokes—say "fuck," and you got a following.
Say "fuck the government," you got the college circuit and amphi-
theaters.

      You think I was gonna go up against that? Forget-about-it.
Whatimy, nuts?

      Excuse me. *(to waitress)* Honey, can you get me another
one a these? *(holds up his glass)* And one for my friend here. But
not so much ice this time. And eight-six the little umbrellas, okay
doll? Thanks.

      (returning) So where was I? Oh yeah, money. Big money.
So for the big money, I got smart and got outta stand-up. Went into
artist management. I got offices New York and L.A. We handle
comics both coasts. But... But the bottom line is, big money's the
Mother of us all. You have it—you sleep like a baby. You
don't—you're up all night crying; worrying about car payments.

THE BIG POOL

Bullshit.   Money's like mothers milk—a nipple—soft, warm, relaxing.

And honestly, could the two of us be sitting here, yakkin' away like this, poolside, mid-day, a place like this, with a cocktail in our hands, if it weren't for Mother Money? Course not!

(Sits up) And unless I'm mistaken about you, pal, you weren't born with a silver spoon any more than I was, right? *(pause)* I thought so. I read people. And like me, I bet you worked your fucken ass off. Bustin' your balls, eating shit along the way, kissing asses— whatever! The whole nine yards—right? Until that *golden* day— when some big deal clicked! And the doors opened. And you got that car, remember? That beautiful car you always wanted. And you finally found youself in the drivers seat, goin' down that road, looking out your windows, watching all the slaves out there working their butts off. And you knew...you had arrived.

(throws ice cube in the air, catches it in his mouth— chewing) Hard work! Hard work and *sucking* up. That's it. The American Dream, right? And we played, and we won. We *won*, buddy. And now we got the spoils a war.

You want a cigar? *(pause)* No? You're right. S'a bad habit. *(puts out cigar in ashtray)* Smelly. Stinks.

Alright. So where are we? Cut to the chase and come in for the finish. We're the victors reaping the well deserved benefits of our efforts. Sharing it with our beautiful wives over there. Watching them splash away in the pool, in their itsy-bitsy bathing suits, and dark, dark tans. Paradise.

And speakin' of wives, I couldn't help but to admire yours. Some doll. Whatta bod. Top of the line. Yum-yum, you hit the jackpot. What's she, twenty-two, twenty-three? *(pause)* NO! No. You little cradle robber you. That young? Well score one for your team.

My Stephie's twenty-four. Not bad huh?—for an *older* woman. She hits that health club every day to keep that bod like

4

that.

Yes, we are lucky. Lucky men with our kewpie doll wives, frivolous as they are. Splashing away. Always spending. Cutsie kewpies. Prizes. Gifts from heaven. The rewards for our hard work.

So...anyway, hows about you and yours come join me and mine, up at our suite, for some drinks—have a little party. Get outta this sun. We gotta view that'll knock your eyes out. Throw some dirty movies on the VCR, get comfy, play some games. Have some fun. Whatiya say? *(pause)* Great! Okay. I see you got that look. That smile of mischief and merriment. And I told ya, I read people. And you, you're a lover of new adventures. And your gonna love my Stephie—she's some...entertainer. Take it from me. We're gonna have some party. And Stephie really puts out...for company. And after all— what are vacations for? To meet people—get together. A few drinks—a good time. We work hard—we play harder!

And as soon as that fucken waitress gets back with our drinks, we can pull our little fishies out of the pool, and mosey up to my place for some real fun. *(Puts another ice cube in his mouth, chews and smiles)* So...tell me...tell me...what's your wife's name?

ETHAN

Ethan - 30's-50's - A street
Rebelling against a society he felt was too constricting, Ethan
became a loner. He describes what he does, what he thinks, and
where he goes during a typical day in his life.

ETHAN: Between these headphones,
    Behind my sunglasses,
    And underneath this silly hat,
    There's a world that I own;
        Where I live quite alone.
            And feel so much,
                so deeply.
    I sit
        in the corner of a small restaurtant.
        At a table
            by myself.
    I nibble salad,
        sip some wine.
        Read my book while I dine.
        With an occasional look,
            my eyes dash to see
                who surrounds me here.
    But then I scurry back to my book.
    Because after that look,
            I remember with whom I'd like to be. ME!
    And after the meal,
            a quiet stroll down the street.
            S'like floating on air,
                with nobody there.
            Turn on the walkman,
                haven't a care.
    Hey!... I know I'm unusual,
            because people always stare, and...
                I don't know... Maybe it's my clothes,

6

ETHAN

or these buttons I wear.
Or maybe it's the way I walk,
like "forget it. I don't care!"
But in any event,
I'm glad I'm here,
making waves in the ocean of
lemmings
By myself in the water,
Balanced on a log.
Going through my life
holding steady.
Living with the freedom of the solitary drift.
On the street,
any beach,
I'm always "beyond reach."
Just one,
a single,
among so many.
Look, I've fought in the damn army,
and served time in jail.
Yeah,
sure, sure,
I was closed in,
grouped out,
like a piece a manure.
Without an identity,
Number this,
or that.
Always next in line,
everything down pat!
Perfect!
In order!
The organizational mould
of church, state, and country,

ETHAN

Every law we're supposed to
uphold.
And keep to the constitution
of *We* the people, WE!
Well GOD DAMN,
SON OF A BITCH,
THERE WASN'T ROOM FOR ME!
In that
claustraphobic,
fenced in,
faceless society.
And so... I bolted! Out!
Disappeared.
Left the ranks of man.
With just my headphones,
these sunglasses,
And of course
this tin can...
That always seems to get filled
by the end of every day.
Certainly's not due
to anything I ever say
to those people passing by.
But they keep putting their coins in.
Although I haven't a clue, why.
I just sit and watch,
and in it drops,
like money from the sky.
FREEDOM! FREEDOM! I'M INDEPENDENT!
Then...back in my room,
no sound but mine.
No clock,
or radio,
or phone.

ETHAN

Even here,
    in my home,
        I want to be alone,
            without the distraction of humanity.
So I can play all night,
    with my tiny toy people on the floor.
        Little soldiers,
            with little cannons.
                Winning battles
                  in my wars.
GOD! I'M GOD HERE...
        to my hundreds of toy people.
        The little families,
            and castles.
                and churches with steeples.
I move an arm
    and a village is gone.
But I'm a good King.
    Yes, the Royal Monarch Supreme!
    And I am the power that be.
Yes,
I am a good King,
    and a good God.
But most of all,
    alone,
        here in my room,
            I am free
            I am FREE!

RAPHAEL

Raphael - 20's - Broadway, near Times Square
Raphael recounts to his buddy Nino the earth shattering drug
experience he had the night before.

RAPHAEL: *(Explosive)* From my chest Nino! Right here. Right
here by my heart! You jus' left. Went downtown to score some
more from Carlos, remember? An' ahm jus' gettin' off. Nice little
buzz, y'know? Nice. Lookin' at the lights; feelin' good, y'know?
Then I felt it man—ZING!   Like all of a sudden. Eruptin' from
right here. Felt like I was havin' a fuckin' heart attack a somethin'!
My chest starts poundin'—BOOM! BOOM! An' then man...then
it opened up. I swear. It fuckin' opened like in that movie, Alien.
Y'know wit' that thing comin' out. This was no heart attack man.
No. It was... *(softly)* Yo Nino, it was a bridge. You hear me?
WAS A FUCKIN' BRIDGE! Hel—lo! Right here. Times Square—
last night. I swear to Christ. A bridge. A wooden bridge.
Y'know, like ya walk over. Over lakes a somethin'. These grey
wooden planks is poppin' outta me. One-after-another. I'm shittin'!
I'm fuckin' dyin'! I'm screamin' for my life! 'Cause I never seen
nothin' like it. 'An it keeps comin' an comin' like a fuckin'
accordion a somethin'—openin' up, unfoldin' outta me.

Okay. Okay, alright. So I'm tryin' to hold this thing. But
you know how big a bridge is man? S'fucken' GARGANTUOUS!
But people still be jus' walkin' by. Y'know, like nothin'. Like
nothin's happenin' here. Nobody noticed, right? Fuckin' city! An'
this thing keeps comin' out. Comin' an' comin'. Stretchin' all the
way down fuckin' corner over there. By the bus stop. See where
that guy's standin'? *(He points)* Over there, yeah. Way the fuck
over there. An' nobody noticed, right? Here I am, fuckin' bridge
comin' outta me, you'd think somebody at least stop. Or look. Say
somethin' like, "Isn't that odd? That chap over there's got some
kina bridge growin' outta him." But no! Nothin'! No one! No one
even stopped. You could *die* here, people walk right over you.

Well it's still comin' out, an' ahm still freakin', but all of a sudden I notice somethin'. Way down, other end a my bridge, I see a babe.

 This woman *standin'* on my bridge. Nice. Sweet. An' she starts comin' towards me. Arms open. Like this y'know? Brown hair, nice bod, sweet lookin'. An' what's weird is I could feel her, man, walkin' on my bridge. An' that's a strange feelin'. Very. Believe me. An' as she's comin' closer, I say to myself, I know her. This chick, this babe, I know her from somewhere. I call out, "Yo miss! You on my bridge, call a cop! Yo Miss! Please, nine-one-one!." But she keeps comin' like she didn't hear me. "Yo miss, please! Help, will ya?!" Nothin', she keeps comin'. Walkin' right up to me until we're like face to face. I know her! An' she's wearin' this blue kerchief, an' she takes it off, an' puts it around my neck like she use ta. Puts her arms around me an' kisses me on my cheek. I remembered man! She says, "Raphael." I say, "Yo!" She says, "Raphael, don't do drugs. Just say no!" *(a beat)* Was MY MOTHER, MAN! MY MOTHER! Y'know that picture I got by my bed. Her holdin' me when I was a kid. That picture taken right before she died? Was her! But she wasn't dead! She looked jus' like when I was five years old. Like time stopped. PEAKIN' MAN! FUCKIN' PEAKIN'! An' she's kissin' me all over—my face, my head, like ahm the best little boy. Like she did back in my room when I was a kid; right before I go to sleep. Kissin' me all over. But then, just' like nothin—she stopped. What happened?! An' she starts 'backin' away. "Where ya goin', mama?" She starts like leavin' me. "Yo mama! Mama, where ya goin'?" An' she's wavin' her finger like this, sayin', Don't! Don't! Don't! "MAMA! HEY MAMA!" I grabbed for her and that's when it happened. The bridge... My bridge started comin' down. Rippin' outta me. An' people on the street started screamin'. Got crazy. An' the pain man...the bridge rippin' outta me. The pain! I thought I was gonna die. An' people are screamin' everywhere. Traffic stopped. Buses beepin'. Wood fallin' everywhere. Was like the end of the world man. Chaos! An' my mama...was gone. She like disappeared.

RAPHAEL

Gone!

Next thing, there's ambulances, fire engines all over the fuckin' place. Times Square insanity! People all over! An' the doctors are lookin' down at me. Somehow I ended up at Roosevelt Emergency. An' they're yellin', "WHAT'CHA TAKE?! What pills? TELL US!? What pills?"

"Where's my moma?", I said. "Hey, where's my bridge? Wha' happened?" Nobody answered. Then it went dark—zero. I don't know what the fuck they did, Pumped my stomach a somethin'. I dunno. Jus' got out couple a hours ago. I am wasted man. Hate those places. Wiped out.

So that's what happened. Some fuckin' story, huh? *(He takes out the blue kerchief, ties it around his neck)* Unbelievable! But it happened, I swear. What'd we take man? What was that shit? Brings 'em back from the fuckin' dead. That stuff brought my mama back. Nino, what was it? Can we cop some more? Huh? Yo Nino, c'mon. Let's get some more. Go downtown, get some-more. Okay? Come on Nino. Yeah? Okay? Yeah!

TOMMY

Tommy - 30's-50's - Anywhere
Every Friday night Tommy leaves his wife and family in New
Jersey and sneaks into New York for some hot sex with street
hookers.

TOMMY: So you're over the bridge and into the city. Off a the
street, and inta a rhythm with some bitch that spits love for a couple
a bucks. An' I know when they're fakin' it. I'm no fuckin' idiot.
Times like that ya wanna smack these bitches hard and get ya
moneys worth. They think just 'cause you're in from Jersey, you
don't know better. Well, I can tell them a thing a two. A FUCK'S
A FUCK—no matta' where ya from. An' they shouldn't fuck with
a dick, unless they know how to do it. See, I got a load that's ready
ta shoot, an' these bitches are playin' doll house with my dick like
I got all day. My wife could do it better!

So I'll let 'em play around with it for a while, until finally
I lose it an' throw 'em outta the fuckin' car. S'a waste a my time.
"Here bitch, take ya fuckin' money an' go fuck yourself, 'cause
nobody else will! First learn how ta screw an' then sell it."

Y'know it pisses my balls. Pisses my balls a lot wastin' my
time like that. What! Don't they think I know when I'm bein'
jerked off?! Whatta my, a fuckin' virgin or somethin'?!

So... I"ll cruise around a while. An' like there's a God in
heaven you can always count on there bein' a bitch on a corner
tryin' ta make a buck. I'll stop the car. Check her out. Give her
the eye. She'll do her "Goin' out?" number, show me her tits, and
I'll say, "Yeah, come on." An' in she'll pop, an' off we'll go.

An' I swear ta Christ, it never fuckin' fails. Sooner or later
you always get the right one. That one wet smackin' bitch that's
primed an' ready ta squirt. An' that's heaven man. Pure heaven!
When that hits, it makes the ride over from Jersey, the time, the
money, all worth it. It all clicks. Ya know what you're there for—
ta get laid by a good fuck. When you get that one bitch who knows
how to suck a dick— What can I say?! There are no words.

13

TOMMY

S'like...a religious experience right in the front seat a your car. When she goes down on you, those hot lips... You close your eyes, and let the wonders of her mouth take you off. An' you never want it to end... But a course it does.

So her you'll tip an extra ten. Zip it up, out she'll go, and off you float all the way back to Jersey. But that whole ride back, s'like she's still there with you, sittin' in the front seat a your car, suckin' your dick. While your head's up in heaven, an' you're higher than God.

THE BEST DILEMMA

Robert - 40's-60's - A waiting room
Robert is one of the wealthiest, most successful men in the world. However, Robert yearns for anonymity—to be just one of the guys.

ROBERT: Yes...I am... I am... I...I know that...or I should say, I've been told...that...I look different in person. Better, right? Better than in the photographs. Perhaps you've seen them. Somewhere. The tabloids...or on T.V., whatever. But that's...

What I'd like to say... Talk about... Clarify, really is... Who I am. I mean... That is... Me. Me, the person. The fellow behind all those photos that people are always looking at... So often. Or those interviews. Or the press you've seen or heard about me...over the years. I am...well...it's that... Well, to start off from the very get-go... I am...horribly bothered. It has not been easy... being me. No. Yes, in some ways my life...has been like an ordeal. Yes. A total, neverending dilemma.

It has been, oddly enough, quite the opposite of what I appear to be in all of those magazines. I am...really very different than what you think I am. That is...well...when you begin your life, as I did... Why, even my name, Top. Zenith Top. Well that was it, from the very beginning. And no matter how hard I have tried, and I have, believe me. I was somehow...placed.

The events in my life seemed to have cradled me... Imprisoned me really, on a shelf of fame and notoriety, and...such unimaginable success, that...no matter what I did, or... Simply put... I have always, always been the *best*. The best! The very best at everything. Not a minute of a day without a rave, or a clamor announcing how "best" I was. How...eventually, I was destined to become the leader of the kids, president of the classes, head of all the corporations, etcetera.

Going back to my earliest memories...the other kids' mothers abandoning them on the street, just to hold me for a minute.

As a toddler in the sandbox, the other children, begging for

15

my attention, would build giant sand castles for me, or give me all their toys, or fight with each other just to play with me.

I went to parocial school, and the nuns always chose me to play Jesus in the school pageants. And at Christmas time, I always played both God and Jesus in the Nativity plays.

I never studied for school. I wrote scribblings on paper, handed them in as homework, and always got A or A+, or better. Always better. Better than everyone. Always the best. The best grades, the best friends, the best girls, then the best women. Perfect—everything. Every minute, always, all the time. Day in, day out. It has been horrible!

There have always been so many, many friends, all around the world, constantly calling me to come for visits and to "hang out" for as long as I wanted.

The phone calls from all my admirers—everywhere needing my approval and opinions.

I am Zenith Top, and I have done nothing but walk through my life and there have always been garlands at my feet and looks of awe. When all I have ever really wanted was... I don't know, perhaps...a small flat somehere...far away...quiet...a cup of coffee... a book... That's all. I'd be perfectly content.... Really.

The villas that I own, the estates, the corporations, the money, the fame... It is all some sort of mistake. I don't want any of it!

We all have... My dream is...to run off to Rumania, or Czechoslovakia perhaps. Live in a small, obscure village of peasants... Clean chimneys, or be a janitor. Melt unnoticed into the local scene. Unobtrussive... Unspecial... Mediocre. Just...sit at home, every night watching T.V. Go to sleep... Wake up... Make mistakes. Not always be liked. Unimportant. Unnoticed. Fallible!

I am Zenith Top, and I am not! But... But...if I am the top—then in my world, the top is the bottom. And most is least. And those poor people who struggle and claw to make it to the peak are...wasting their time. I have seen them, and watch them suffer.

THE BEST DILEMMA

I know them. A great many of them are my friends here, and we... console each other every day.

I am... Please... Just because I wear these raggy clothes, don't be fooled. I have more money than God. I know, because he is a personal friend, and we are...inseperable. He comes for little visits, on Sundays, like you do.

I know. I know. I can tell. Yes. It's time, isn't it? You have to leave. I understand. It's a long drive. Please, please, by all means, go. With my blessings. But remember, now...we... you...know me now. Don't you? Thank you so much for listening. Sometimes, I talk too much. And, please...my best...to everyone... out there...outside...in the world.

SID

Sid - middle aged - a crowded restaurant at lunch time
Sid, a scheming, aggressive, New York talent agent, has
recently experienced his partner's death in their office. While
at lunch with his future son-in-law, he weaves the story of the
death scene into a plan he has for his son-in-law's future.

SID: *(He's eating a pickle in quick, little bites. He's middle-aged.
A little overweight. Loud and agressive.)* All ya gotta remember.
All ya gotta remember Lenny is... Red meat books! Dead meat
doesn't! And they're always called "talent," Lenny. "Talent." And
in the office you're always nice to everyone. Even the go-fers. You
need 'em. Secretaries too. Love 'em like family or at least... let
'em think you do. Y'know, pretend a little. Little insincere
sincerity. The business is based on it.

And be aware that whatever you say, it may come back to
haunt you. S'like karma or something, I don't know. Let the talent
talk. Let 'em. Agents whisper—softly, carefully. 'Cause even a
crack, a slip, a wrong word accidentally spewed at some
unimportant, half-assed, has-been, can come back years later to
haunt you. Yeah. I know. I've seen it. I've been there.

You'll be at a cocktail party or something. Some uh...actor
you once said boo to hundred years ago will remember, make a
scene, throw a drink, embarrass you. Ruin your night. Happens all
the time. So eyes open—mouth shut. They're not your enemies, no,
but they're not your friends, either. They're talent. Talent, Lenny.
And talent either books or doesn't. Simple. Red meat. Dead meat.

(to waitress) Carmen, honey. *(to Lenny)* Excuse me. *(to
waitress)* Where's my roast beef-rye-rare? I'm starving here. Well,
could you get it for me sweetheart. Thank you. *(looks at his
watch—then up at her, throws her a kiss good-bye, back to Lenny)*
Nice tits, huh?

So anyway... I get to the agency this morning. And he's
crazy. Fuckin' crazy. Nuts. Nuts. I don't know why. Some L.A.
deal with Tri-Star. Something went kaput. But as usual, what! I

18

get the grief. Y'know, gas the Jew like it's my fuckin' fault.

(then) You gonna eat that salad Lenny? Oh. Okay. Ga' head. No-no-no. Ga' head. I was just... No, eat! Eat Leonard! Eat your food. Mine's coming. Any year.

(back to story) So. I said, "Nick. Nicky. Boss. What is it?! What are you carrying on about? What? Tell me." But he's erupting like this shit means something. It doesn't. You know that, Lenny. This business is bullshit. Bullshitizola. A game, y'know. Who's dick's bigger—wins. We all try, but if not today, then it'll be tomorrow. Fuck it. End of the day. Ya tally up. See which actors booked. Drop some of the losers and leave. Forget about work. Go out, have a couple a drinks, shmooze in some Eighth Avenue dive. If ya lucky, get laid, then go home to the family— have dinner, watch TV, pet the kids, kiss the wife and go to sleep. Pleasant dreams.

Next day s'a whole new ballgame. And that's it, Lenny. That's it in a nutshell, the talent biz.

You still with me? Good.

So... Nick goes in his office, slams the door. SLAM! Next thing he's on the phone—yellin'. Screamin' like a fish wife. "You mother fucker this! Son of a bitch that! I'll ruin you in this business!" Oy! Got a mouth like a toilet. But it's his agency, right? He can say or do whatever the fuck he likes.

So he's blah-blah-blah. Blah-blah-blah. Then all of a sudden, nothing. Nothing! Quiet. Gets very quiet in there. He's never quiet. Never! Then I hear the phone drop. A "help" like moan. A gasp. Then a fall to the floor. I get up. What!? Run to his room. He's on the floor, Lenny. Looks terrible. Like green, yellow. Eyes popping, y'know?

"What! What can I do for you, Nick? Tell me." He looks up. Tries to talk. But his eyes go back in his head. I check his pulse—he's dead. Dead. Just like that. In *my* arms. *(looks at his arms)* These arms, Len.

(then) You want some salad dressing for that? No. What,

just oil and vinegar? Good for you.

(then back to story)

So... Anyway... I sit there with him for a while. Get up, collapse in his chair. He's got a big, expensive leather chair. Take a breath. Look around. He's got a big office, Nick. Nice. Impressive. Expensive things. The best. Dial 911—report it and sit there. And while waiting...while waiting, Len, I start thinking about life. Crazy, huh? Yeah, life. All of it. Work, the family. My daughter, Connie. Two of you getting married soon. You bein' outta work. Needing a job. And a light went on, y'know. Called you right then and there and set up lunch.

Cops came—took him away. Funeral's tomorrow. S'terrible. S'terrible. *(then)* I don't know. What can I say? Can you start the day after? We're gettin' busy. S'comin' into pilot season. Lotta work. Good money. Yeah? Great! It'll be nice havin' someone in the family in the office. You can give me, the new boss, a little moral support. And I can keep an eye on you for my little princess. Make sure you don't fool around on her. *(Laughing)* Just kidding. Kidding!

But in all sincerity, Leonard, I'm really glad you're comin' aboard. I am. I really am. And I mean that. I do, from the bottom of my heart. *(then)* So...uh...tell me, you gonna finish that salad or are you just playing with it?

LARRY

Larry - 20's-40's - Anywhere
Since their first meeting, Larry and his wife have always had
very intense feelings for each other. The intensity of those
feelings have, on occassion, gone out of control. One evening
the passion of their love almost destroyed them.

LARRY: We didn't go to the piano bar that night. Why? Well,
we'd been having so many fights lately, that we could hardly stand
to be with each other anymore. Anywhere, even in the same room.
One fight after another. Over anything. Nothing. A tremendous
strain on our marriage. A wound spreading. I felt it and she did
too. So we stayed home that night, see? To have this talk. A
summit.

We sat in the kitchen, at the table, directly across from each
other. We had trouble getting it started. We were both tense—
nervous. So we avoided—skirted every issue going back as far as
our first date. All this shit pouring out! Unresolved everything! It
seemed like, alright, okay, it's over! Our marriage has been a big
mistake. A bad deal. Fuck it! But we couldn't let it go. Some
thread of something tied us together. Held us in some dark place
that we couldn't get out of.

We couldn't talk anymore without erupting. So finally I got
up and left the table. She followed me, and started getting crazy—
cursing at me. And I was getting angrier—furious. My fists were
clenched. I wanted to turn around and belt her. Bash her face in.
And she started jabbing me with her words—her accusations. I was
yelling. She was screaming. Then she stood in front of me, defiant,
and slapped me in the face as hard as she could.

(softly. intense.) I froze. I fuckin' froze! At that moment
I wanted to kill her. Rip her apart. We were like animals—ready
to attack. Destroy, kill each other. Our eyes connected in rage.
Love was hate. Heaven was hell. And I wanted to choke the life
out of her. My hands going towards her throat, and I was yelling,
"WHY?! WHY?! THIS IS BULLSHIT! BULLSHIT!!"

LARRY

Then she grabbed a sharp knife out of the drawer, pointed it at me, and said, "Come near me and I'll kill you! I'll kill you!" We stood there. Just stood there. Hate—hating. Checkmate— FUCK YOU!

(soft. intense.) I said, "Put that knife away."

She said, "No."

I looked at her, ready to kill me. That look on her face. I looked at myself, ready to kill her. Then I...sat down at the table, looked at her, and said, "What are we doin? This is insane. What's happened? WHAT'S HAPPENED TO US?!"

She looked at me, terrified, dropped the knife on the table, and slowly walked away. Far away. To the other side of the kitchen. The distance between us filled with emptiness. And then... she started to cry. I've never heard anybody cry like that; in so much pain. And I felt it. I felt her pain! Do you understand? And I got up and went to her. I needed to...hold her. I needed... And she looked at me, and we held each other. And cried together on the kitchen floor—openly, deeply. Like children. And she said, "I love you." And I said, "I love you." And we didn't say another word. *(a beat)* That night...when we made love, it was... a celebration!

EDWARD

Edward - Any age - Edward's desk
For a writer, getting writer's block is always a painful,
frustrating experience. For Edward it's a nightmare that is
frighteningly real.

EDWARD: Gray skies on an inkblot night.
Finding that phrase that will say it.
That word in the niche...
That thought that I crave...
It alludes and drifts, somewhere in the air.
Damn it! Come down to the page.

Say it as I want it to be said.
Don't whistle in the air.
Please come here and let me put you to rest.

But no! It stays illusive and I suffer.

So I pace and turn,
And rip through the night.
But where is that phrase?
I can't find the words.

DAMN IT! COME DOWN TO THIS PAGE!

So I throw myself down on the floor, enraged.
And I beat my fists till I bleed.
And I pull at my hair,
And rip off my clothes,
Tearing all papers,
Then breaking all pens,
As that phrase comes seductively by.
And taunts me—for not being quick enough.
And feathers my brow.

23

EDWARD

And kootchies a koo.
As I lunge for those words,
But they zap to the Bronx,
Leaving me
> Wordless,
>> In need,
>>> And now nude.

This is War!
> Right!
>> Fuckin' WAR!
I pick up the pens (that are broken).
I lift one of the crumpled papers from the floor.
I go to my desk,
> sit rigid with conviction.
Intent to confront,
But armed with a pen.
When those words come playfully by (and GIGGLE!)
The nerve!
I feign indifference by doodling.
> Pretending.
"Not thinking of anything at all, ya little bastards. Just
sitting here, as usual, naked at my desk. Doodling, that's
all. Can't you see?"
So they sneak closer.
But I continue to doodle.
Closer.
Still doodling.
Closer.
Doodle.
Then... I fake a disinterested yawn.
And, HA!
> They foolishly overstep their bounds.
I carefully lift my broken pen to the crumpled doodled sheet.

EDWARD

And then...
　　　　　　　the event!
　　　　　　　　　The miracle occurs!
Those words,
　　　　those expressive little pictures,
　　　　　　　appear to me
　　　　　　　　　in a phrase
　　　　　　　　　　　that I jot down
　　　　　　　　　　　　　in ecstasy!
Unblocked! Unblocked!
As the flow begins.
Thoughts into words on the page.
I write in delight all through the night,
　　　　　　　　　　in a joyful,
　　　　　　　　　　　　naked,
　　　　　　　　　　　　　　abandon.

JOSÉ

José - 20's-30's - A street
José, a drug addict, had a beautiful vision of heaven last night.
He tells another junkie what he saw.

JOSÉ: Wuz like...wuz like it wasn't the streets no more. You hear
me? Was like it wuz heaven. An Carmen an Pino, they wuz angels.
Angels! An we wuz so fuckin' happy. All of us. No shit. Not
even fucked up. Nothin'. Just hangin' out, like in this nice place.
Cooled out. Not dirty. *Everything* man, *everything!*

An I didn't need ta score no shit there. No. Nothin. I just
walked aroun' in this beautiful place—holdin' this crufix, an did Hail
Marys, like for rushes. Can ya dig it? Was *beautiful* man,
beautiful!

An I saw everyone who died. An they looked great. Shit!
Not strung out. Smilin'...smilin' like after some big score.

An I wanna say. People wuz nice. No sucker shit. No
fuck overs. Oh! You shoulda been there man! Wuz like a fuckin'
dream.

An I saw Big Jack an Angelo. An get this, they wuz
smilin'. Now, can you imagine—Big Jack smilin'? Fuckin' goof
ahm tellin' ya. Right? It was *high!*

An I felt so good. Inside, ya know? Like high, but not
high. Like clear—unfucked up. Not needin' no shit. Nothin'. Jus'
cool. Straight. Straight—an' cool. Shit!

But mostly, like it was so clean. So *clean* man. Not a piece
a paper anywhere. Imagine! You hear me?! I FELT SO CLEAN
INSIDE! So fuckin', FUCKIN' CLEAN! GOD!

SAL

Sal - 30's-50's - Sal's All Night West Side Diner
Sal, the owner of a diner, thought he'd seen it all. But one
night, a strange little man came into his diner and literally shook
the place up.

SAL: He wanted home fried potatoes, that's all. I don't know. I
remember, he came in here lookin' like anybody else. Short guy.
Sat at the counter. Right over there. I asked him, "Yeah, what'll
it be?" And he said, "Home fried potatoes." Nothin' unusual. No
big deal. So I ordered up with Sam, my short order cook. An I
turn around, and this guy's like smiling. Not unusual. But...there's
like this green glow comin' offa him. Yeah. That's the best way I
can put it. Right then and there I knew somethin' strange was
happenin'. Now listen, we get all kinds comin' in here. Two, three
in the morning we get truckers, drag queens, hookers, but none of
'em, none of 'em ever glows with green rays comin' out of 'em.

So, I kept it together, said, "Excuse me...um, is there
somethin' else I can get'cha...besides the potatoes? An he stopped
smilin. He was like staring. Intense. Like he was studying me or
somethin'. He looked at me like...like I was some kina insect.
Creepy. Very creepy! If I wasn't the only one behind this counter,
shit I woulda jumped an ran. But the boss woulda killed me for
leavin' the register.

Now there were a couple of regulars at the counter, drinkin'
their coffee, oblivious to the whole thing. Wheras I was freaked!
I never seen anybody glow. Ever! An it kept gettin' brighter and
brighter.

I was tryin' to keep my composure. But I was fallin' apart.

Then, we get like into this starin' match. Him an me. An
even though he's not sayin' anything I can *hear* his thoughts. Yeah.
An he was sayin' some weird shit. Stuff like a computer. Yeah.
Like, "The population of New York is... The size of the city...
Elected officials are." All this data shit.

An ahm gettin' so scared I think ahm gonna shit in my

pants. I didn't know what to do. Should I call 911? My wife? My mother? The army?

An this guy's glow is gettin' brighter and brighter. Takin' over the whole diner. This green shit's coverin' everything.

Finally, I say, "Hey Mister, your fries should be ready in a minute. Ya want something to drink, like coffee or somethin'."

Then he screams in this high pitched tone, "Coffee?! Coffee?! You mean caffeine? Caffeine?!"

I said, "Uh...uh, we got decaffeinated if you like, or tea... or somethin'. I don't know."

Then his green shit gets brighter, and floods the place. Guys at the counter, they fell over backwards. I figured they was dead.

I lost it. I screamed, "Mama mia, whatiya doin' mister? Ya food'll be ready in a minute. Please! Stop!"

Then the whole diner starts to shake. Yeah. Like it was an earthquake. Dishes flyin' all over the fuckin' place. Sam comes running outa the kitchen, screamin', "What the hell...," but when he sees this guy, he turns and runs back in, leaving me alone, face to to face, with *it*. Whatever *it* was.

An then his face starts contorting in these weird ways, like it's made of rubber. Its mouth opens wide, an out comes this long pointy, yellow tongue. An this tongue starts comin' at me. Long and pointy and sharp. An the place is shakin' like crazy. I...

Finally, I totally freaked! I said, "Enough! Enough! Get that fuckin' tongue back in your mouth, and get the hell outa here! Now! Who the hell you think you are!" I felt so strong. Like I wanted to wave a flag or somethin'.

At first, nothin' happened. But then, the place stopped shaking and calmed down. My heart was racing like crazy, but I stood there locked, with my fists like clenched. Then I pointed to the door and said, very softly, "Get out."

And the green rays zapped back into his body. And he pulled that tongue of his back in. His face stopped contortin', and he looked like anybody else.

But then, he kina slumped over in his seat, looking dejected or somethin'. He put a buck on the counter for the home fries, which he never got, an said, almost in a whisper, "Thank you. Thank you very much, sir." And he started to leave.

I stood there, still shakin', an said, "Sure. You're welcome. You're welcome." And then, he left.

MELVIN

Melvin - 20's-40's - Forty-Second Street
Melvin lives a Jekyll-Hyde existance. During the day he's Mr.
Stein, a proper and respectable teacher. On weekends he's a
pill-popping drug addict who runs around Times Square like a
mad man.

MELVIN: *(Wearing heavy duty, slightly sleazy 42nd Street clothes.
He's twisted and having a great time.)*
    I'm cruisin' on the fringe.
    Like hoppin' on my brain's tail.
    I'm *stoned* on the weekend.
        Yeah, I'm *stoned* here on the street.
    Where everyone looks
            psychedelically tourist
            in pastel greens *(snaps his fingers)*
        Yeah—now lavender blues.
    (abruptly sincere) And I'm loving you.
        I am.   I do.
(a quick reverse) But who...?
        gives a shit! (he laughs)
Right?!   Right?!   Right?!
        Cause there's a *zip* through my earlobes
        that's connecting all the dots.
That I left behind in Brooklyn
        on the drive in tonight. Dot-dot-dot.
      Or was it out? Dot-dot-dot. In out, in, out.
Can't remember.
(trying to remember) Can't, cause...?
            Can't, cause...?
(remembering) Cause I dropped some fuckin' acid.
        That's why!
      And now I'm hangin' with the brothers.
          Shitfaced high!
Jive-ass cool.

MELVIN

No longer Mr. Stein;
         the only honkey in the school.
That's behind me.
In the school room.
That's a gonner until Monday.
No more kiddies.
No more classes.
                    I got shades now—see?!
Blaster blastin'.
Cuttin' fringe.
And goin' hard core.
Neon lights,
               and scumbag thoughts.
Pussy talkin'
and pistol whippin'.
(trying to be ultra-cool)
"What-cha-watchin'-mother-fucker?!
Can't-cha-see-just-who-I-am?
Can't-you-see?
               Or don'cha know?
Hot-from-cool
                    mother fucker!!
                         Dig it!
I'm da teacher of your children. Yeah.
    Cool, huh?
               Mighty fine. Mighty fine.
But Monday through Friday I'm,
               "Mr. Stein!" "Mr. Stein!"
Here on weekends I drop some drugs
               and all pretenses.
Lose my mind—but not my senses.
Cool as shit. Yeah!
With egg fried brains.
    I escape like a sleazoid in

the night.
No more blue class collars
strangling too tight.
(like a crazy uncle)
So keep your kiddies off the streets, folks.
Cause I get 'em every Monday.
And I teach 'em, yeah, what the book says.
(angry) But the book don't say!
THE BOOKS DON'T SAY WHAT
AMERICAN IS...
I KNOW MOTHER FUCK'UH WHAT AMERICA
IS!
And that's it.
That's why,
I,
Mr. Jive-ass Cool,
get a life,
escape the lies
that I teach each day in school.
So it's not the texts man,
or the talks.
See, the crack in the blackboard jungle is real!
Oh, it's real!
S'yall come and visit.
But don't forget your acid.
S'the only way left you can still feel.
Cause the system's a drain, man.
It's a bust!
But out here on the streets
are all the people.
And the people man—
is us!

JOHN

John - 20's-40's - A dark street
On his way home from work, John is mugged. As his life and
death struggle with the mugger unfolds, John learns a great deal
about who he is and his power to survive.

JOHN:
"Whatiya want? Huh? Whatiya want?!
You want my wallet? Is that it? My wallet?"
And he says, "Yeah."
"Well okay." I say, "Here."
"Take it. You got it. You got it all. Now let me go."
And he says,"No."
    Then presses his knife to my throat.
I say,
    "What?
        Whatiya want?
            You got it all. That's all I own.
                Just... just leave me alone. Okay? Okay?!"
    As he's sweating—dripping. His eyes are like rocks, and
they're staring at my throat.
"No.   Don't.   Please!
        I got kids," I say.
    "So what!" he says. "So what!"
Eye to eye.
Knife to throat.
There we are.
"Don't," I say. "Please don't. Please!"
    But inside...
        But inside there's a "No!" growing.
                    "No!" growing.
        "NO!"   "NO!"   "NO!"
And the sound is bigger than the two of us.
On this street,

33

JOHN

In this city,
Acting out,
About to die.
But filled,
      So filled with rage,
            That I howl from the top of my life,
"NO! NO! WHO THE FUCK DO YOU THINK YOU ARE?!"
And I push,
And I hit.
And I kick so hard from the bottom of my life,
            that his knife goes flying.
      So I slam him down on the street.
Kicking!
Kicking!
      Then I grab my wallet,
          and spit,
              on this piece of shit below me;
               Who's begging now.
As he covers his face.
And cries for his life.
As I'm holding his knife,
        And I stand there... staring.
      Till the cops come.
      Sirens and lights.
      Helmets and guns.
        Finally finishing this scene that we started.
As they read him his rights,
         then throw him in the car.
And I go to him.
Look in the window.
He looks back—frightened.
And I stand there.
We stare through the glass.
Until I look away.

JOHN

And start to cry,
        and break down.
'Cause I can't understand, "Why?"
      Why did this happen?
        On this night,
            Between the two of us,
           Him and I,
               Strangers...
                  in the city.

JOE

Joe - 30's-40's - A neighborhood bar
All his life Joe wanted the American dream—home, wife,
family. When his dream becomes a reality, it is more than he
can handle. One night, while spending a quiet evening with the
family, Joe has a major anxiety attack and leaves. Later, he
tries to understand what has happened.

JOE: *(highly charged—on the edge)* Who'd ever thought, right!
S'like Norman Rockwell—America! Kids. House. Everything.
Shit!

On Saturday nights, Chinese food...the kids fighting over
spare-ribs. Half the neighborhood's over, I get gas, T.V.'s blastin'.
S'nutty. It's nutty. I never thought...in my whole life...eveh.
D'chu? Huh? When you knew me...way back when...when?... half
a million years ago... Would'chu ever have guessed then...that
some day I'd have the whole sha-bang? Like this... Huh?...
Never... Right? Some detour I took from then!

An my kids... You seen 'em. They're fuckin' gorgeous.
Right?!

An my wife, huh?! A *stunner*! Knockout. An let me tell
ya... That woman... She's there for me hand an foot. An me, I
would kill for her. I love her so much. *(pause)*

So what! What about it, right? Why even talk. Well...ahl
tell ya... Ahl tell ya... *(pause)* Tonight... I hadda get outta there.
I...I couldn't breathe. It was...wellin' up in me. All that *love* there.
So good. So...an it's all mine. I have it, ya know? An all I have
to do is... I don' know. I don' *know* what I have to do. I was
sittin' there in the livin' room. I look around. Kids are playin'.
She's in the kitchen cookin'. An at that moment... It was *everything*
I ever wanted. Ever! And... I couldn't handle it. It was *too* good.
Perfect. My life... Perfect! Everything! An suddenly I couldn't
breathe. I got nuts...an bolted. Ran out the door. An I kept
running. Kin you believe it? I went fuckin' crazy! Outta my mind.
But... But it's over now. Ahm okay. I...I just...needed to talk.

JOE

That's all. Yeah. Thanks. Ahl be fine. Ahl go back soon. Crazy, huh! It'll be okay. Anyway. Yeah. S'enough. Over. *(pause)* So...tell me...what about chu? How you been doin?

VINCE

Vince - 40's-50's - A police car
Vince, a New York City cop, has just been assigned a new
partner—his brother Joey. As the two drive through a dangerous
neighborhood together, Vince prepares Joey for the rough times
ahead.

VINCE: They're fucken animals and that's all. Remember that!
Think of it that way. And each night when we drive through here,
just remember, we're in a jungle with wild animals; but we have our
guns. Simple. Simple. It's no more than that, no less. There's no
adventure or mystery here, okay? That's for T.V. and the movies.
You wanta make believe, then go to a movie. 'Cause when you're
working here with me, this is real. It is. And always remember—
we work in a combat zone. And in a combat zone, Joey, ya fight
and ya kill. And later on, when you're home at night with your
wife, then—there—you can make love and be tender; and come back
to the gentle part a yourself. But never here. And never ever
confuse these two things, Joey, please. Please don't, okay? Because
there's no way you can make nice when you're fighting for your life.
You can't. You can't soften even for a second. Not with them.
Not here. Because if you do, Joey, if you do, at that moment these
sick fuckers'll know it. They...they'll see it in your eyes. They
smell it. And it's just what they've been waiting for.

    (pointing) Make a right here. On the corner. Slow. Go
slow. Okay.

    And...uh...and at that moment, Joey, *believe* me; believe me
like there's a Christ in heaven, they'll fuck you—royal—with a knife
in ya heart. And that'll be the end of the party. No more dancing—
ever! I'll have lost a brother, Jeannie'll be a widow, and you'll be
one dead cop! *(giving directions)* Slow... Go slow down here.
Make a right. Good.

    And...there'll be one happy jungle bunny out there that
night; celebratin' with the rest of them crack heads. They do that,
ya know? They have a party when they kill a cop. They... *(giving*

directions) Shine the light! Over there! See that. Over there. That alley. They call it Paradise Alley. It's where they all shoot up. Always check it for action. Okay. S'empty. Keep goin', slow.

See that guy. Over there... Him... One who's waving to us. He's Mr. Big Dealer on this block. I always wave back to him. *(he waves)* He gets a big kick out of it. *(under his breath. fake smile. looking out window.)* Hello yourself, you dumb son of a bitch. Don't worry, we'll get you someday. Keep wavin'. You'll get yours. We'll get'chu. *(back to partner)* He loves this waving shit. Makes him feel like we're friends. Like we wouldn't down each other in a second. I'll wave. *(waves)* Yeah, I'll wave when he's behind fuckin' bars. I'll really wave then. And it's a bitch to bust him 'cause he never carries. But we will. Let him wave. We'll get him. And Joey, never turn your back on him. Ever. Not for a second. He's poison.

Let's pull over here, by the meter... Hang out awhile... Catch the action... Somethin'll go down. S'early. But it's Friday, and the animals get hungry on the weekends. And sooner or later they'll crawl outta their trees for some food. All we gotta do is sit and wait. There's always somebody sellin'.

So... So baby bro', how ya likin' it so far? Fun, huh? We just gotta wait for party time. We're the uninvited guests. They'll be out; in all their colors. *(pause)*

Do me a favor...huh...please, stay alive—okay?... And... don't forget to call mama on Friday. It's her birthday.

MICHAEL

Michael - 30's-50's - A street

Even though he had a successful career in business, Michael chose to chuck it all and move to New York to live the life of a bum. Now, free of worry and all pressure, he describes the many joys and adventures of the lifestyle he finds so satisfying.

MICHAEL: *(sharing—joyful—with a drunken, childlike abandon)*
>And in the morning,
>I leave my grassy rest in the park.
>And explore.
>And scout the city.
>This beautiful, beautiful city.
>My best friend.
>I survey all terrains—unprejudiced.
>And nickle-bottle my breakfast in deposits for food.
>Or I'll eat whatever the garbage cans will allow.
>Depending on the generosity of others.
>Because...I killed pride last Thursday.
>Now I can eat anything.
>It all goes down the same.
>My stomach'll say: "So what!
>>It's food.
>>It fills.
>>There's more to life than just
>>>desserts."
>And after that, a cigarette butt on the curb.
>And I linger around thinkin'...indefinitely.
>"What new adventure today? Where?
>Uptown? Um...East Village? Um...Bowery? Um..." and

on and on.
>Thinkin' all out to my heart's content,
>And however long it takes until I swagger up a dream.
>Then slow-walk it,
>Or become a subway stow-away.
>Location... Undetermind.
>>>And Unimportant.

40

MICHAEL

'Cause when ya there...ya there—and that's it.
And out goes the cap.
Ya put on the pity,
And if they're out there and kind and ready...
Ya always get the change for the bottle.
Thunderbird,
Or Ripple—cherry flavored or straight.
Then I pull up a piece of curb,
Toast whoever passes by.
"Hello! Hello!"
And I sing to the city.
Sing out!
Whatever song hits me.
As loud as I please.
No more...Beverly Hills Hotels.
Or shmoozy deals.
Pressure cooked,
With ulcer lived lives.
Knife stabbing everywhere.
'Gone.
And left behind.
Anothere lifetime.
I'm now a free agent.
No secretaries.
No schedules.
No time clock life.
And...I love it! Love it!
This city affords me...myself.
And I afford myself the luxury of living...fully.
And on the lam.
So I drink to you.
        And you.
        And you.
        And you.
        That you, too,
        May all find yours.

BIG A

Big A - 30's-60's - A bar
After discovering his wife and another man in bed together, Big
A drives into the city to get drunk.

BIG A: *(He is about forty-five years old, wearing an expensive
business suit. The top button of his shirt is open, his tie is loose,
and looks a bit distraught. He is half-sitting, half-standing on the
bar stool, and is holding a near empty glass of scotch. He is
animated and aggressive.)* MORE! Much, much more. Like I was
saying, I was rolling around in the ring with the money people. And
I mean up there. Big six figures. Exec. V.P. at a Fortune Five
Hundred, you see?

(looking at glass, then up at bartender) Another. Little less
soda please. No ice. That's fine. Thanks. *(back to story)*
Everything. EVERYTHING I COULD WANT! Right? House in
the country—Connecticut. A classy wife—blonde, blue eyes. Two
picture-perfect kids—*not* on drugs. And all of us living in palatial
spendor. S'perfect. The American Dream, right? Okay?

But when you're that rich, you gotta protect it. 'Cause if
you don't, if not, it may be stolen—piece by piece. Your rainbow
can collapse. Your pots a gold gone. Stolen by who? WHO? Ha!
Some fuckin' thief in the night, that's who. A man you never met,
but he knows all about you. And he hates that you have, and wants
what you own. That's by who.

Okay. Okay, so whatiya do?

First you hire security guards—they walk and watch. Next,
watch dogs are bought. But they can't be played with because they
bite.

Then—you put twenty g's down on some cockamamie,
fancy-shmantzy, does-everything-but-suck-your-dick burglar alarm
system. So that now you feel protected, your ass is covered, your
portion of Paradise is safe and secure. Right? Am I right? You
following me? I hope so. Because what I learned is, some things...
(finishes his drink) Gimme another please. Ga head. Fill it to

42

the top. Thanks. *(continuing)* Some things...are unprotectable. No matter who you are. No matter how rich.

What I'm saying is dreams—all dreams—are distortions. Not reflections—distortions. Distortions! Okay, so what does that mean? Huh? What am I talking about?

So one day you arrogantly walk into your half a million dollar home, as I did today; and there she is—your classy blonde wife, in the den, going down on her private, probably bisexual, fifty dollar an hour, aerobics instructor. You watch in shock as I did. They see you and stop. EVERYTHING STOPS! Everything! And all I could say was, *(meekly)* "Uh... Hi honey, I'm home."

Then you dissolve. Somehow end up alone on a chair in the dining room, looking down the mile-long table, at the sunset outside the window.

I thought about my kids, work, things I've fought for all my life. And when I was all thought out, I walked. Opened my eyes and stopped the dream. Closed the door—and left. Got in the car—drove. Kept driving. Got to the city, found a bar, this one. And am now sitting here with you having a drink. Or is it my third? Sitting here, watching you watch me. Listening to me go on about... SHE WAS ON HER KNEES MAN! HER FUCKIN' KNEES!! My wife! Mine! Giving pleasure to a man I never met. And from what I saw, he was being...satisfied. And I felt like fuckin' death. Empty. Dead. Comprende?!

Because...he had everything. Not just the sex, or my wife. What I saw...he was...he looked satisfied. Satisfied! You understand?

The wheel of fortune goes round. And things change. Instantly.

Mister Bartender. Sir.

And what was important, isn't any more. And what wasn't— is.

Do I still love my wife? Yes, I think so. Do I hate her right now? More that you can imagine. Should I stay here, in this bar? Keep drinking? Go home? I don't know. I don't. All I know is every dream has a price. You pay. And to win you gotta lose. Ya gotta.

(*softly*) You...wanna give me another. Please. Sir! One more. For the road...back home. The last one, okay? Do me a favor. This time fill it all the way—to the top. (*He looks up at the bartender*) Yes, please. Right...to the top.

TONY

Tony - 20's-30's - Anywhere
Tony, a blue collar worker, thinks of himself as quite a romantic catch. However, he never seems to last in any relationship. He laments to a close friend how his last girlfriend did him wrong.

TONY: I said, "Honey, this is it. I decided like, from now on. I'm gonna be totally honest with you. No more games. Level out, open up, and be real with you."

She looks at me and says, *(mimicking her)* "Are you kiddin'!" Then she starts ta laugh.

"What's so funny?" I said. Like this is a hard one for me. But at least I'm willin' to make the bend. I mean lookit, I know we haven't been goin' out long, but still, I think s'time for us to start thinkin' like about a more serious kina relationship. Yeah, right, like even marriage and kids, da-da, da-da, da-da.

"Get off it!" she says. And starts laughin' even louder.

"How can you laugh?" I says. "Here I am, Mr. Nice Guy, humbling myself, throwin' my guts at your feet, plannin' on being like Mr. and Mrs. Paternal-Maternal. And to boot on the thing, to boot! I'm even willin' to make a good woman outta you. And you have..."

But before I even finished my sentence, she stops laughin' and glares at me, *(mimicking her)* "Make a what? Make a good woman outta me?"

"Yeah, ya know, make ya Mrs. Respectable. Marriage. The mother of my..."

But again she hits me with, *(mimicking)* "MAKE A GOOD WOMAN OUTTA ME?!"

At this point, I'm detecting some slight anger in her voice.
"Yeah, by the rules. The book."

(mimicking her) "In case you haven't noticed. I *am* a good woman."

"Yeah, sure. I guess you're good." *(trying to joke)* "But'cha can always be better, honey."

(mimicking) "Better'n what!?" she says, getting outta the bed.

45

TONY

Now, I was beginning to feel somewhat fenced in, if ya know what I mean.

But again she hits me with, "Better'n what?!"

I see this can'a worms poppin' way too fast.

(trying to clam her) "Baby. Honey. Relax. Lookat, you're a good woman. I'm a good man. We're good people. Now come back in bed. Let's drop it. And when you get back here, I'll show ya good. C'mere."

"EAT SHIT, YOU PRICK!" she says, startin' to get dressed.

"Where the hell you goin'? What happened? Lookit, all I was tryin' to do was COM-MUN-ICATE my feelings like you're always asking me to do. Now look'a this shit!"

(mocking) "You can communicate your bullshit feelings with another bimbo buddy. I'm leaving."

Well, I wasn't gonna stand for that number.

"Okay, then. Leave. Anytime I want I can have kids with anyone else. And I got news for you, lady. You'd be a god-dam shitty mother anyway!"

She finishes dressing. Storms over to my bed, and hits me with, *(mocking)* "YOU ARE ONE BONAFIDE WOMAN-HATING, SON OF A BITCH, PRICK!"

(smug) I didn't say a word. I didn't have to. I just sat there, in bed, ignoring her.

Then she slammed the door and left. I thought to myself, "WHAT THE FUCK WAS THAT ABOUT!?" Ya know, ya try to be honest with them. Tell 'em the truth, now look a this shit. WHO THE FUCK NEEDS 'EM!!

So... I like cool out for a moment. Relaxed. Relaxed. Have a cigarette, take out my telephone book. Call this girl, Mindy, I know.

(Mr. Charm) "Hey Mindy, how ya doin' baby? S'*me*. Tony. Mr. T. What ya up to tonight? Why don'cha come over? Yeah, it's a little late, but I'm all alone. I've been thinking about 'cha. I miss ya. I wanna talk to you about somethin'. Come on over. I'll tell ya when ya get here. Hurry up. I'm waitin'.

PRINCE

Prince - 30's-40's - A street

Prince thinks of himself as the smoothest pimp in town. He strolls down Eighth Avenue, beginning his nightly search for some new, young "talent."

PRINCE: *(Dreamy and druggy—with a slow, sensuous rhythm)*
Slinkin' on a bus stop sign.
Eyes are like lead, can't make it to the top.
Someone yells out, "You're a bookend."
An' I say, "Yeah, but I'm alive inside."
An' the summer night breeze just blows me away.
Blows me away.
Blows me away.
It's a setup for a good time—Ah haaa.
S'a setup for a good time.
So I stroll down the street like the Bob Shu Bop King.
With a razzle de dazzle.
And a Bob Shu Bop.
It's the night of a *thousand* stars.
Ah haaa.
Walkin' the street.
With my eyes on my feet.
Which are goin' in two different ways—Oh nooo.
Over and under,
In a slow motion thunder,
Goin' down to the curb,
And then...
A crowd.
Lookin' for life below,
That's me.
Lookin' for life below.
So I wiggle a finger.
With a "Hi" of a smile.
An' move it around to show 'em "life lives."

47

PRINCE

An' up on my feet,
Ahm back on the street.
An' I walk through the crowd,
Towards the Greyhound.

(accelerating)
Little black girls at the bus stop jive.
Little black girls make me money.
Ahm the King of the street,
An' the Prince of the Fair.
Two snorts later an' my head is all clear.
I'm pushin' a strut,
An' up in the air.
LET'S MAKE MONEY!

C'mon little girl, d'chever hear a Sister Kate?
Listen up girl, I made her great.
Am the one who did it.
I made her a star.
A hundred a night.
An' more in a car.
The tricks are simple.
They're goddam easy.
There's nothin' bad, or sick, or sleazy.
Let me be your Daddy.
Ahm a cool ass Dude.
You're under my wing.
Ahm here for you.

(slowly and gentle)
Don't be afraid.
Ahl protect ya from the dark.
There's angels on my shoulders with flashlights.
An' they're lightin' up the night.

PRINCE

An' open up the bedroom for the Money Man.
Take my hand, little girl.
Daddy's home.
An' you're sittin' in his pocket.
Right by his heart.
Sittin' in his pocket,
An' he loves ya, ah haaa.
Loves ya baby-baby.
Love ya.
Loves ya baby-baby.
Loves ya.

HARRIS

Harris - 20's - A bar

Harris just can't figure out why he never seems to score with the ladies. The way he sees it he's doing everything right but nothing seems to pay off. Awaiting the arrival of a blind date, he looks for some last minute reassurance from a close friend.

HARRIS: *(with growing desperation)* Look, don't worry about it, okay?! I won't pounce on her. Believe me, last night was enough. I learned my lesson. Look, you saw her, right? She looked like a mover, didn't she? I figured, hey! She's good for some koo-koo-ka-chew, right? Okay? But what, just like always, slam-bam-out! I never got to first base; or anything passed, "Hello...my name is", to her "Who gives a rap?! Get lost!" Which made me feel like shit. Like I wanted to disappear from the planet, crawl under a bar stool.

I DON'T UNDERSTAND THEM!! Is there something I'm missing here? Look, you know me. You've seen me in action. I'm a smooth operator, right? Am I missing a turn somewhere? There some flaw in my social technique? What gives? What?!

I mean, I do the basic, ya know, "Hello... How do you do?"...cha-cha-cha. But they look at me like I'm not speaking English.

Hey, can you blame me for getting so discouraged. When I look ahead, my future looks so bleak and lonely, it cringes my skin just to imagine. What! Eighty years old and still trying to score at some senior citizens bar, right next to the I Never Got Married Nursing Home. NO! I gotta get it together. Now! Tonight! I know I'm still young, but look, my track record is...non-existant. Zero! But I don't feel desperate or anything. NO! This time it's gonna happen. Tonight. With your friend. Whoever she is. You'll see. When she walks in that door, there'll be a new me... Mr. Studly on the goove. Right?

So...where is she?! C'mon, I can't wait. How do I look? It's crazy, but all of a sudden I feel like I can't handle this. Like... I don't believe in myself. Isn't that nuts! But I'm okay, right? Sure. You believe in me don'cha? Don'cha?!

50

RALPH

Ralph - 20's-30's - A bar
Once again Ralph met the perfect girl. In the middle of their
two day sexual marathon the strangest thing happened; they
accidentally had a moment of genuine intimacy.

RALPH: *(With a growing erotic excitement)* I looked at her and
said, "You...are evil." And she laughed. So I laughed. Then she
looked at me like she did back at the bar. Y'know, "that way." And
I just melted. Total defrost! Those eyes a hers infilltrated my
cerebellum, and I mozeyed into her lips, full packed, and thirsty for
some stuff.

She smiled, said, "Sloooow down," and pulled her head
back, like this, y'know? And man, we went at it for hours. Hours!

Then, she told me how nuts I was. So, I'd grin my dumb
grin, like a God-damn fool. Say something like, "Yeah, I guess I
am."

An' I'd try gettin' real with her by sayin', "Who are you?"
But again she'd give me that coy look.

Then we drank some shit like apple wine, I think. Or
smoked a joint, I dunno. And we'd go at it again. And again!

So that night collided into the next day, and backed up into
another. I mean we just hung out like that—losin' it completely!
Lovin' it! But losin' it. Drifting from one plane to another. Every
second bein' spiced with an erotic sound or whimper. Hers! Mine!
I dunno! That coy look. Then a frantic rhythm, steady. Together.
Then KABOOM! Around we'd go again. Licking, sweating,
touching. Hot. Hot! Kiss.

Then at one point, my eyes caught hers...so unprotected.
She looked...so fragile...and sad...and lonely.

I ast, "Hey, you okay?"

She tried to smile, but couldn't. We stared into each other
like that for a long time.

And then she ast, "Are you okay?"

I said, "I don't know. Hey, what's happenin' here?"

RALPH

Then, we both began to relax. Really, really relax. Totally let go. We held each other, like in a way we never had before. The room seemed so big all of a sudden. And so dark. We were like two little kids holdin' each other real tight. An' we stayed like that. Didn't say another word all that night. Right into the next day.

I'm tellin' ya, I had a connection with this broad that was outta this world, and it wouldn't stop. An' it wasn't just that animal passion; or the dark, down, and dirty stuff.

Our souls was doin' a loop-de-loop, y'hear me? Our auras was bouncin' off the walls. And twas not just the grass or the booze. I mean, the way she looked at me. Like I was the only star in the galacti! And I felt like King Shit Supreme!

Yeah, this one was for real. Total! Completemente! Perfectzione! Shit, whatta fuckin' scene!!

LEFTY

Lefty - 30's-50's - Anywhere
Lefty's been having sex with prostitutes for years. Here he describes the night he got more than he bargained for in a life and death scene with a hooker in a cheap hotel room.

LEFTY: It was a cartoon set up, y'know? She wanted fifty bucks. I had the fifty. She's clean. It's a buy, turn the page.

Alright, so she's hot, black, maybe twenty, twenty-two. Who could tell? So we begin the parade in bed. Her floats a poppin', we're rockin' an' rollin'; when from nowhere, I mean NOWHERE, she pulls out a knife. I'm tellin' ya—a KNIFE!

I said, "Wow! Very kinky baby."

She says, "Kinky yo' ass daddy. Give me yo' cash."

"You're kiddin?" I said.

"Cash! Now!"

Well I get up like ta split. An' she jabs me!... With the knife!... In the back! With a rip!

I'm numb. I don't believe what's happenin'. My life starts speedin' by me on a revolvin' door. She takes a powder. An' BOOM! It hits me, I'm gonna die!

Here I am, alone in this sleazy hotel room somewhere, bleedin' Niagara on dirty sheets...an' like this is it. S'over. Right?! End a the line. Last stop on the chu-chu. Grand total. Here's ya bill sir. An' lights a goin' on, as they're goin' off. An I break down an' cry like a baby. An' it goes dark. Kaput!

Next thing, some white shirts, bright lights, an' the doc's are sayin' what a lucky man I am. How I jus' made it. Another minute more... An' they sew me up.

What can I say?... What can I say afta' somethin' like that, huh? Huh?! Ya life changes. Bran' new view a things, y'know? What's important. What's not. All the bullshit. Yeah.

But the bottom line, and end result is I'm still here. Yeah. I'm ALIVE! *(A beat)* Funny story, huh?

53

PIANO MAN

Piano Man - 30's-50's - Anywhere
Piano Man couldn't stand it anymore. Everywhere he looked he
saw moral decay, filth, and perversion. One night in a church
he expresses his feelings to Jesus.

PIANO MAN: *(with growing frustration—he is in conflict)* I was
talkin' ta Jesus last night. He was sittin' by himself up at that
church on 49th off Eighth. Ya know, the one with the big gate in
the front.

Whatta... Whatta nice guy he is. But I hadda ask... Jesus,
whatta-che-do? Why'cha let this stuff happen? Look...looka' whatta
mess we got here. The hookers, an' drugs, an' disease, an' pimps
all over. Whad happened? Please tell me what went wrong? Who?
Who did this? Why?

He looked beautiful. I swear I never saw a man to look so
beautiful. Ya know...the...the...beard and that hair.

So Jesus said, "It's gonna be okay."

I said, "How can you say this?! If you saw the garbage in
these people—the filth in their hearts, you wouldn't say this."

Then he puts his hand on my shoulder—very comforting.
Ya know, the guy's got hands like porcelain.

And he says, "The good has to lie with the bad, in the same
bed." That got me! What are you talkin' about Jesus? Ahm talkin'
about the disease in their souls. An' you're sayin' 'Good and Bad
in Bed?' That doesn't answer it. Now tell me, whatta we gonna
do?! How we gonna clean it up?! Come on, let's do somethin'!
What?!"

"Let it alone. It'll be okay," he says.

"Jee-sus have you seen Eighth Avenue?! Have you seen
what's on those streets?! Listen to me. I know what I'm talkin'
about. I've seen it all out there. An' all you can say is 'let it be.'
I can't!! It's gotta change! We gotta change it! C'mon, make a
miracle! Get God to help you!"

So he looks at me with those big, sad eyes. And just looks

an' looks an' says, "Let them be there. They need to be there. They've *got* to be there."

"What! Jesus," I said, "What ya talkin' about? We *need* a miracle. Look around. Jesus, please! Help me, Jesus, please! The place is falling apart!"

An' all he would say is, "Good is there. Good is there. Good is there. Look for it."

I looked at him. What could I say? I don't know. We sat down in one of the pews. He had this lovely smile on his face. Man's got a great smile. I just kinda gave up on the whole thing. Whatta Messiah!

He said, "Let's pray."

"Okay Jesus, you're the boss."

And so we sat there last night—two guys in a church, praying.

HELEN

Helen - Middle-aged - Anywhere
Her husband Morty is asleep, so it's another night of T.V. and
boredom for Helen. Hearing a knock on the door, Helen
answers and meets her tiny new neighbor, Hal, and her life
changes forever. She recalls that first meeting.

HELEN: *(Middle-aged, robust, with a sense of fun and well-being)*
It's the craziest thing. It is. Don't ask. I'm sitting home another
night—bored. Dozing off, watching T.V., Morty's in the bedroom—
asleep, as usual. And I'm just drifting off when I hear this sound,
like a pin or something, knocking at the door—"ping-ping." I
thought I was dreaming. But then I heard it again, "ping-ping."
Who the hell's that at this hour? So I get up, turn off the T.V., go
to the door.
"Who is it?"
No answer. I wait a second.
Another little knock. "Ping."
"Who's there?"
Again—nothing. Another "ping." I peek through the peep-
hole. No one. I put the chain on the door so I could take a safe
look. These days ya never know. And me, I trust no one. No one.
Slowly I open the door just a crack. *(she does)* Nobody! Then I
hear this...this "voice." *(she does a squeaky voice)* "Hello. Hello!"
I look down and there's this TINY little man. I mean small! Two
inches—tops! This big. *(she shows how big)* And if he weighed
half a pound it was a lot. My mouth dropped. And he's smiling—
very nonchalant, smoking a tiny cigarette. As cute as a button,
debonair, wearing a little turtleneck, a smoking jacket, moustache.
Very elegant. Like Ronald Coleman.
And he says, *(squeaky voice)* "I hope I haven't bothered
you. I'm your new next-door neighbor—Hal. Hi!"
"Well, hi Hal," I said. Took the chain off, opened the door,
bent down and shook his little hand. Adorable! "Nice to meet
you." I didn't know if I should invite him in. But since Morty was

home, what the hell! I said, "Come on in." And in he came. I showed him around the apartment, making sure not to wake Morty. I couldn't get over how SMALL he was.

We went in the kitchen for coffee. I lifted him up, put him on the table. I'll tell ya, it feels very strange to have a man in the palm of your hands like that. Very!

And we're sitting and chatting, and he's charming. He's sitting on the edge of my saucer eating the tiny crumbs from the coffee cake, while I sipped my coffee and listened. And he told me all about his life. And whatta life!

His parents were in the circus, they beat him all the time. So he ran away. Lived on his own for years. Poor thing. Slept in drainpipes, hid in fields of grass, fought animals and insects all the time. A life of *constant terror*, I'm *telling you*. But like Hal said, "I made it! I survived! Little me!"

Eventually he got in some kina school somewhere, and now he's in computers. I mean "in" computers. He works inside a them. Fixes them for big companies. Lotta money. He makes a lotta money.

And as he's talking, I'm thinking—there's a strange man in my kitchen. And y'know I found him—very attractive! Very handsome. And that tight little body—very sexy! Every once in a while our eyes...connected—just for a second. I'd blush and look away. *(she does)*

He was so attentive to me. So polite. I wasn't used to that. Certainly not with Morty. Never.

But mostly we just talked. For hours. His life, my life, his lonliness, mine—with Morty. We found we had a lot in common. A lot!

Then, at one point, I'm putting my cup back in the saucer, and he stood up, and grabbed my little finger with both of his hands. We looked at each other, and then slowly he started to like "caress" it, stroking it. It felt so good—wonderful. Warm. I said, "No Hal, don't! This is wrong. I'm a married woman."

Then he gently kissed my little finger with his little lips, and whispered, "But are you happy Helen? Are you?!" Then he rubbed his chin all the way down my finger, right to the very nail—and kissed it... A wave went through me. WOW!

I pulled my finger out from him; nearly knocking him off the saucer. "NO HAL, WE CAN'T! Not like this. A one-night stand. NO! You'd better leave... Please."

He looked so sad, hurt. "That's not what I want. You got me all wrong Helen."

I said, "Do I? Do I really, Hal? Do I look like I was born yesterday? C'mon, I know men. You're all alike. I let you in my house, it's late, we're alone in my kitchen. I know a pass when I see it."

"But you don't know ME," he said.

Maybe he was right. Maybe I was wrong. I said, "Ya better leave, Hal. This train's goin' too fast for me."

I picked him up off the table, put him on the floor, and we slowly walked to the door... *(she stops herself)*

When we got there, I opened it, looked away. He gently touched my toe, said, "I didn't mean to hurt you Helen. I'm not that kina guy."

I didn't say anything.

"Can I kiss ya goodbye? Please?"

I said, "No." But then very softly I said, "Sure." And then bent down, picked him up, and held him in front of me—face to face. He smiled. I tried to look away, but he gently grabbed my bottom lip in his hands and kissed me. Those little lips on mine sent a charge right through my body; I almost dropped him.

"You're somethin'," he said.

"So are you mister." I put him on the floor, leaned on the door, and said, "Seeeya tomorrow."

He kissed my toe, winked and then left.

I leaned in the doorway. Thought about Morty, our marriage. And then I thought about little Hal. And everything became razor sharp clear.

Well...to make a long story—short. I saw Hal a lot after that—almost every day. And well, we fell in love. Crazy, huh? But I'd been so unhappy with Morty for so long, and Hal was my way out—and I loved him! But the bottom line, I realized—it's only love that satisfies. Not a man's SIZE.

And as crazy as it seems, we're leaving for South America tonight. Gonna start a whole new life. Look, I'm nobody's fool, I know what's ahead of me, it'll be rough. But what the hell, WHAT THE HELL!, ya only live once, right? And it's like that old Beatles song, *All You Need is Love*.

(determined) And we're gonna make it! *Wait, you'll see!!*
(a beat, softly) Anyway, that's it...the story of Hal and me.

LILA

Lila - 40's-50's - Anywhere
Lila, an earthy exotic dancer, has spent much of her life desperately looking for a man. Along the way her dancing career began to plummet as she accepted one sleazy job after another. She recalls how the events in her life lead her to an epiphany one night in a cheap club in New Jersey.

LILA: *(exuberant)* Kidding? No. I'm not. I'm not kidding. I did. I danced on Hullabaloo, on T.V., in the sixties. I was one of the *original* Hullaballo go-go girls. I was. If you ever saw the show, you saw me. You hadda. Yeah. I was in the go-go cage; short black skirt, clinging sweater—tight, always. And my eyes darkened heavy with mascara and eyeliner—giving me that Egyptian look. And my hair, teased up a foot high, and locked in laquer.

Dancing—Always dancing. Keeping the beat. Wiggling away. Doin' the jerk, the frug, the monkey. I was a non-stop hell-za-fire turning on the millions of Americans, our viewing public, every Tuesday night. Burning! Shaking my hips—my lips puckered, like this. My arms open, inviting, stretched out, like Diana Ross. I was seducing the country.

Then, towards the end of each show, I'd zero in with my eyes, direct my gaze, like this—right into that camera lens. Feeling so sexy and turned on. And what I'd do is, I'd imagine that one man, sitting home alone, watching me on T.V., being turned on, wanting me. And looking right into that camera, I'd think, seductively, "Call me, baby. Call me." And I'd dance just for him. Give it everything. For him, my fantasy man with a key, who'd free me from my Hullabaloo go-go cage.

Well, it turns out, Mr. Fantasy never called.

And after the show went off the air, I started working all the go-go clubs around town. The cages got smaller, and so did my costume. But one thing was still the same. Each night, when I'd hit my light in the cage, and started dancing, all those eyes on me, I'd turn it on, full steam. Jiggle-jiggle shake.

And I'd work that room, looking for him, the man with the key. 'Cause now I wanted out. The fun was gone. "Call me. Call me."

The only ones that ever did call were the sleazos and creeps. Forget it!

Go-go came and went. And so did I. The years passed. The clubs got smaller, raunchier. My costume just about disappeared. And my only music was a drum. Ba-boom.

I became "Miss Lila Lee Vine, the Ice Maiden," locked in her cage. I was drinking a lot. Falling apart. My looks became stares. My "call me's" were more desperate.

It was a new club; some dive in Jersey. My first time there. Time for my set, but I was drunk. I made it up to the cage somehow, and got in.

The drum started. A slow, soft beat. Boom ba-boom, boom. I was a hungry lioness in a cage—prowling, while working the room. Looking for prey, while dancing so slowly. Boom, ba-boom, boom. Stalking. Looking through the bars of my cage, for the right eyes, the man, boom-ba-boom.

Then, I noticed the other dancer. Across the room, in the other cage, some tired old hag. I got her attention. We danced to each other in our cages, above the room. Our movements—slow, together. The drum got louder, faster, BOOM-BA-BOOM! BOOM-BA-BOOM! I smiled. She smiled back. The beat picked up even more, BOOM-BA-BOOM! We were in perfect rhythm, but all the eyes in the bar were on me. I danced that night, like I never danced before. Never! Not even on Hullabaloo. And she copied me, my go-go partner, step for step. I started grabbing at the bars of my cage, wildly! So did she! I waved. She waved back! I started laughing. So did she! We were... She... Something... She... she... She was me!! It was a mirror!! It was... I had been dancing with myself. And it was me, all along! And I...started to laugh. It was tremendous! Funny! A joke! Hysterical! All my life it was her. She was me. And it just seemed so funny. Everything did. Even the men in the bar started laughing. It was crazy. You

shoulda seen me. I was like outta control. Totally possessed—
dancing with myself in the mirror. And...I didn't even care if I was
sexy anymore! Yeah, or anything. It didn't matter. The best night
of my life in a dive in Jersey. *(pause)* Well pretty soon I stopped
dancing, for good. I stopped because... I don't know... I suppose
because I didn't need to anymore.

MYRA

Myra - Middle-aged - A tenement apartment
Alone another night, Myra dreams up a romantic evening for
herself. In tonight's fantasy, she is Lotte Lenya, adored and
lusted after by a young soldier during the war.

MYRA: *(Kurt Weil songs play softly in the background—She is
earthy, sultry, experienced)*
    I'm in a... I'm in a Lotte Lenya kina mood.
    Sexy. German—very German.
    Putting on my nylons,
            sitting by the window,
                listening to Kurt Weil.
    Looking at the moon.
        "Hello moon."
    Wearing just a corset and a smile.
        On this warm night.
            A good night
                for a sailor.
    One who's young—not tired from fighting in the war.
    The kinda Johnny that likes his girls
                slightly ripe and mature.
    Our eyes will say "yes." Our bodies will say "sure!"
    And soon he'll rest his head on my bosom for the evening.
    I'll wear my black cap,
            dark skirt,
                high heels, and a tight sweater.
        Enter the bar,
            pull a pose,
                show him how older is better.
    Lean on the door,
        my eyes to the floor,
            and my cigarette lit and dripping;
            And say:
(softly, sexy) "Hello soldier, hello."

MYRA

And through the smoke,
    I'll smile.
Put my hands behind my head,
   Say everything—everything!
      Without anything being said.
A look,
  a laugh,
    the tipping of my hat.
     My Johnny's gonna learn where it's at,
     Tonight in Germany—
       Lotte Lenya style.
He'll ask, "Ya wanna dance?"
I'll say, "The Germans just invaded France.
   But so what! Tonight my Johnny, Let's Tango!"
And off we'll go—
    sexy and slow.
I'll throw my cap on a chair.
We'll dance like Ginger and Astaire.
Our eyes—
  feet—
    touching. Heaven!
Dancing in the dark.
Later,
  a walk through the park,
    on our way back to my place for a
    "nightcap."
"So tell me soldier, how's the war treatin' ya?"
He'll smile. There'll be a mist.
We'll stop.
And of course, we'll kiss.
   Under a street light,
    right downstairs from my place.
(Pointing up) "That's my window. The one with the light.
   Johnny, ya wanna spend the night?"

64

MYRA

I'll light a ciagarette.
He'll smile.
And in a little while,
we'll go to
my room,
my bed,
and music.
LOTTE LENYA SINGING KURT WEIL!
Lit candles,
and no Sig Heil.
We'll leave the war
outside the door.
He'll say,
"I love you lady."
I'll say,
"No Johnny, no.
It's just for tonight.
And then—you go.
Forget me!
Never write,
But Johnny... Oh Johnny, please,
Always remember,
your Lotte Lenya,
and the night you made love...to Kurt Weil."

FLORA

Flora - 40's-50's - New York Port Authority Bus Station
Flora, a waitress, has just escaped from a terribly dull life in the
middle of New Hampshire. This morning she stole away on a
bus to New York. Immediately upon arriving she shares her
story with the first city person she meets.

FLORA: *(The Port Authority Bus Station—3rd floor bus arrival
area—late afternoon. She has high energy, a quick talker.
Enthusiastic.)* The yellow Samsonite! Over there. By the bus.
That one! That's mine! With the little wheels—which didn't help.
I still hadda stop. Damn thing weighs half a ton. It does, but s'my
own fault. It is. I knew. I shoulda been smart, right? But I
overpacked anyway. Cause, well, you don't know me, but once I
make up my mind to do something...like to go. I'm gone. And
there's no stopping me. No sir. And so I packed up this morning,
lock, stock, and everything. Jammed it all into that Samsonite. No
dilly dally halfway moves for me. No sir. And I'm never going
back. Never-ever again. I've arrived! Finally! "Delivered from
Bethlehem!" What? No, Bethlehem, New Hampshire. Everyone
says that. Yeah. Yes, there really is a Bethlehem, New Hampshire.
Believe me. And you never wanna go there, Mister. S'a small town
with small minded people. Small minded and dead, even though
they claim they're still alive. Hidden in the middle of New
Hampshire. Nowheresville. Y'know some days, downtown, there's
not a soul around and those that are, are barely breathing. You gotta
tap 'em to make sure they still are. Well me, I breathe a lot. Deep,
full breaths. *(she does)* And I got tired'a tapping in Bethlehem. So
I left. Got up this morning, jumped outta bed, packed that
Samsonite and I was gone with the wind. No good-byes. Nothin'.
Got on the Greyhound. Closed my eyes and when I opened them,
Bethlehem was no more than a memory. And a bad one at that,
Mister. A weight lifted.

Well, everyone in Bethlehem always said, "Flora, you're
just too fast for us here. You're so New York. You oughta move

66

there someday." Well, they were right, and so here I am in New York, New York. Water seeks it's own and I'm in my element. And... bending your ear, aren't I? Blab-blab-blab. I'm a real talker, right? But...don't it feel like we're not really strangers. Like we're fellow travelers on a road somewhere. Y'know, you're goin', I'm comin'. In transit. Blab-blab-blab. Talk, talk, talk. Why don't you shut up, Flora? Let the man go if he wants to. You're keepin' him from... *(then noticing)* Why... That man's taking my bag. Look. He's... *(to the other man)* Excuse me. Excuse me?! That's *my* bag, Mister! He's got... Mr! That's mine! That's my Samsonite! *(back to the first man)* He... *(notices he's left)* Where'd... Where'd you...?

     (back to thief) Mister! Mister! That's mine! *(running after him)* Stop him! Somebody!! Please!! Stop him! That's...that's my Samsonite! Stop him! Please!

     Somebody! That's...

RUTHIE

Ruthie - Middle-aged - Ruthie's kitchen
Ruthie has been married to Sol, an alcoholic, for nearly thirty
years. He's always been difficult to live with, but recently Sol's
become impossible. Here, Ruthie tells her sister, Pearl, about
a life-threatening scene that's just occurred between Sol and the
family.

RUTHIE: *(She is middled-aged, overweight, bleached blonde)*
"Animals!" he kept yelling. "You're all deceitful, whore-bastard
animals! All a ya! All a ya!" And he jumped up from this table so
fast...so fast, Pearl, I swear, I thought he'd knock it over—dishes
and all. Scared the baby. The baby got so scared she started to cry.
After all, she'd never seen her grandpa carrying on like this. Who
had?! Not me, the girls, none of us. Who could imagine?! We
were stunned! Couldn't believe our eyes. Insanity! Such carryings
on. Was like a scene in a movie. And we sat here—the girls, me;
amazed. Amazed!

Alright, he'd been drinking again. Granted, he was
probably drunk. Who knows! Who can tell anymore? But even
drunk; at his worst, he never carried on like this. Never! Not like
this, Pearl. And why today, huh? Of all days, why today?

I said, "Sol—What?! What's wrong?! Tell me."

And he gave me a look... If looks could kill, I'd be dead in
a coffin six feet under. This wasn't a look you give a wife. It was
a hate look. A murderers look, and it scared me. S'like I didn't
know him anymore.

He got up, threw the chair down, knocked some of the plates
off, and ran over to the uh...to the uh drawer over there by the sink;
opened it, and pulled out a knife. And not just a knife, Pearl—the
big one. The carving knife. The one we use during the holidays.
Imagine! And he stood there waving it. I couldn't get over. He's
standing there in that old ripped undershirt and pants waving that
knife. He looked like some escaped convict on a rampage. And he
kept calling us "whore bastards!" and "bitches." Yeah!

Look, I've been with the man, what, thirty years? In all that

68

time I'd never seen that side of him. Never, Pearl. Over thirty odd
years. I mean you think you know somebody. You do, y'know?
You think you know them inside out. Every inch. But when they
crack, like he did, and you find living within the person you thought
you knew is a disturbed maniac... A horrible... *(softly)* I didn't
know him. There was a crazy man waving a knife in my kitchen.
And me and my girls were hostages.

     Well, Fern started getting hysterical. I mean she'd never
seen her father like this—twenty-eight years. She grabbed for the
baby and started to leave. Escape! But he stopped her. Stood right
in front of the door. Said, "You try to leave, I'll cut both your
throats!" Can you imagine?! A father to a daughter?

     (soft and tense) I said, "Fern, sit down. Sit! He means it."
And she and the baby sat down again. Didn't say a word. Got very
quiet here. Very tense. Even the baby stopped crying. Had like a
smile on her face; the baby. Thought grandpa was playing some
game with us with that knife. So the baby was havin' a ball.

     Finally Delores looks over to me and whispers, "Ma! Ma,
do something!"

     "What can I do?" I said. "What do you want me to do?"

     She said, "Call somebody! Aunt Faye! Aunt Pearl! The
police!"

     But before she finished her sentence, Sol grabs the phone off
the table here, cuts the wires, said, "Ga head! Try it!" Then he
looks at me, says, "Ruthie, you son of a bitch! You betrayed me!
I know all about it." His eyes were bulging. Bulging out of his
head. I thought, okay, any second the man's gonna have another
heart attack. And finally this drama'll be over. But no, he just
stood there staring at us like we were animals in a cage.

     My stomach went from knots to spasms. I said, "Sol,
please, whatta you doin'?! You're wrong! Your daughters came
here today all the way from Queens to pay their respects. It's
Fathers' Day, Sol, Fathers' Day; and you're scaring us. Now put
the knife down. I'll make some fresh coffee. We'll have some
danish. We'll all sit and talk." But no, he just stood there. Kept

saying, "I know. I know, Ruthie. I know all about it."

"What Sol! Whattiya know?!"

He said, "I know they're coming here to take me away. That you're gonna have me committed."

I looked at the girls. They looked at me—Shock!

"Who told you such a thing?!"

"Don't deny it! Don't deny it!," he said. Just then they started knocking at the door. Sol backed into a corner. Started screaming, "Get away! I'm not going! This is my house, and you can't take me away!"

"It's the neighbors Sol. All this commotion." But then he looked at me, said, "How could ya do this?! Ruthie, you're my wife. My wife! You betrayed me!" He kept saying that over and over. "Betrayed! Betrayed!" Was like an echo in here. And the knocking got louder. They were trying to break down the door. And then Sol turns the knife on himself. The blade to his heart. I knew he would do it. I yelled, "Don't Sol, please! Please! I'm sorry. I had too! I had too!" Well thank God, just then, they broke the door in and grabbed him. Got that knife outta his hands. It's a miracle nobody got hurt here. All the screaming and crying that went on. You shouldn't know from it, Pearl. The baby got so scared, she was hysterical. Fern grabbed her and ran out.

Sol was kicking, and biting and screaming until they got him into that jacket. I never knew he was so strong. Took three men. Three big men. And as they're taking him outta here... The look. The look he gave me. The pain, Pearl. The pain I saw in his eyes. S'like I had stabbed him with that knife myself. And again he said, "Betrayer! Betrayer!" I just looked away. I couldn't face him. *(She takes a breath)* I don't know. I don't know, Pearlie. Did we do the right thing? Huh? Did we? I know you never liked him. Said I shouldn't'ta married him. That he's a drunk. No good. But you have to feel for him. And now...now I have nobody. I'm alone like you. And Pearl... Pearlie, what?!... What is it? Why are you smiling?... Pearl! I... Pearl, what's so funny! Pearl!!

WAITRESS

Waitress - 20's-30's - A bar
To help make ends meet the waitress occasionally has sex with
customers from the bar for cash. She describes an unpleasant
scene she had with a crude fat man in the parking lot.

WAITRESS: *(a painful inner monologue)*
    So I said, "Ya wanna?
        Sure?
        Okay. I'm in. We're on.
        But'cha gotta wait till we close. I'll meet'cha in
the parkin' lot. An' don't say nothin' to no one."
    Eh, he looked okay.
        Little fat.
        Little bald.
            I've had worse.
                Payin' less.
        Son of a bitch! Whatta drag!
            Hope it's quick. Hope he's good.
    It's a living.
        Whatta night.
            Whatta life.
                Whatta place.
    So then I said, "You're gonna have to drive me back to my
place after. My mother takes care a the kid. She worries 'bout me,
y'know."
    And he smiled,
        like a snake,
            said, "Sure thing babe."
    An' all I saw were dollar signs.
        And the bills paid.
        And the bills paid.
            Whatta snake.
            Hope it's quick.
            Hope he's good.

WAITRESS

And after that he said,
  "Is the car okay? 'Cause his wife was at their
place. An' a motel cost too much, an' wasn't worth it, time wise.
  "Sure," I hissed. "With you baby, anywhere would be hot
and heaven."
    An' he drooled.
    I swear, he drooled.
    An' my stomach fell out.
    An' my heart sank leagues.
I thought,
    Whatta my doin?
      Such a sleeze. Such a turd.
      I'M BETTER THAN THIS!
But the rent's due.
An' it's winter.
An' I'm cold to my soul.
An' I'm down an' under.
An' I need some lovin'. Any lovin'.
Sides, the cash'll keep me warm.
I'll be warmer in the morning.
    When I forget about tonight.
And the snake man. In the parking lot.
    About four A.M.
    Really alone.
      But with him.
        The snake man.
        The snake man.
        The snake man...and me.

MARY

Mary - 20's-40's - A pick-up bar

Mary gets turned on by meeting men in bars. The man she met last night called himself Captain Midnight.

MARY: He said, "Just call me Captain Midnight, baby."

And so I did.

Then we took a turn around the bar.

And he asked me what I liked.

"Whatiya mean?" I moaned.

"In bed," he said.

"I don't know," I sighed. "Depends on the guy, and the night, and my mood."

"An' just what kina' mood are you in tonight?" he kidded.

"Ahm in a good mood," I laughed. "Ahm in a *very* good mood."

So we looked at each other, and let it melt between us a while. Then he broke the heat by sayin', "Just whatta they call ya back at the ranch, little girl?"

I smiled at him from my bar stool and said, "They call me Wonder Woman, Captain Midnight." And he laughed. I liked how he laughed. I like how he laughed, a lot. And I was warm.

So then we both sipped our drinks to ease the air. But our eyes were givin' it away.

So then he said, "Does Wonder Woman wanna come for a ride with Captain Midnight on his big rocket ship? Ahl fly ya way up to the Milky Way. Whatiya think, babe? Could'cha dig it?"

"Yeah, I could. I really could. But one thing, Captain M. Can we go further than just the old Milky Way? Can we pass the moon, and the stars, and the night? Can you take me over the top? Please? Sir?"

We stopped mid air, and he said, "I got a strong ship lady, with a lot a good fuel. An' if you behave ahl take ya over the top. But it's a long, long night, an' it's time to go... Now!"

"Yes, sir. Ahm ready, Captain!"

Then he took my hand, and I looked up at him. And we left the bar.

And then...we just disappeared.

73

MARIE

Marie - Middle-aged - Marie's kitchen
Marie and Antony have been married for many years. One
night while they're having dinner, Marie sees a ghost come in
the window. Antony is unaware of the ghost. After it leaves,
a terrified Marie tries to explain to Antony what has just
happened.

MARIE: *(highly agitated)* Are you hearin' me Ant'ny. Stop eatin'!
Please. Listen ta me. Please! I swear, on everything holy. It
was...it was like a ghost. A ghost. An' it came in through the
window. Right over there. You just finsished ya pasta, and was
drinkin' a beer. An' I started ta sweat. We're sittin' here, eatin',
havin' dinna' like usual, remembuh? Subway had jus' passed, the
fan was blowin'. An' in it came...like a ghost...middle age.
MIDDLE AGE, Ant'ny! An' I felt it. I did. It like took over me.
Like...a spirit. An' I became old. All of a sudden, very old. Very
old! I don't think ya knew, did'cha?

S'like one minute, ahm *me*, a young woman, servin' my
husband dinna'. We're sittin' here, normal, Friday night, eatin',
like always. But then, everything changed! An' I thought... I
thought I was gonna pass out right here at the table. Yeah!

Then, ya looked at me funny, remembuh? But I... I
couldn't say anything, WHAT?! I was...like possessed. Another
train went by, the curtain was blowin', an' I got up to clear the
dishes. But I still didn't say a word. What could I say?!

I got the cheesecake outta the fridge, cut it, an' served ya.
But by then, I was gone, in a trance. S'like I was in a bubble.

Ya finished the cheesecake, started the coffee, an' looked at
me funny, an' said, "What'sa matta?," remembuh? Ya said,
"Whatta ya cryin' for?" It's like I could finally free myself, burst
through the spell.

It's... middle age. Ant'ny. That's what happened. Right
here! It came in...an'...an'...take care of me! Love me, even if
ahm old! You will. You will wont'cha? Ant'ny? Ant'ny are you
hearin' me!? Ant'ny! Ant'ny! Stop eating! Please! Ant'ny!

74

MARY-ANNE

Mary-Anne - 30's-40's - A street corner
Mary-Anne's just had a few drinks in her neighborhood bar. On
her way home she accidentally stumbles and falls. When she
looks up from the curb, there stands a stranger; Mr. Right.
Mary-Anne awkwardly tries to pick him up.

MARY-ANNE: *(Tightly dressed in black, wearing sunglasses. She
walks briskly, then clumsily falls. She looks up, and sees him—the
man of her dreams, looking down at her. She begins speaking
anxiously, quick chatting)* Oh my! Must have fallen. Never saw
that step. Who put it there? *(Looking up at him)* And they said
chivalry's dead. Thank you. Really. Really. Thank you. Get my
balance. *(getting up)* Get on my feet. *(as she get up her bag opens
and the contents fall out all over the street)* Oh my! Look at that.
The things in a lady's bag. *(picking things up, throwing them in her
bag)* I bet you never knew. Just... Just... I'll be out of your way
in a minute. I'm uh... These...these heels can be enemies to a night
curb. Don't I know! *(Standing up)* Aren't I proof? I must be a
mess. Do you think? Well uh...anyway, I'm up! And uh...thank
you for your time. I know, yes, in this city most would have walked
over me. Literally. Literally!

It's so sad. A woman can't go for a walk anymore. Or
have a drink by herself in a bar if she wants. It's like some rule.
(Coyly) Which I break. I do break that "rule" sometimes.
(Proudly) I like to walk alone. Defiant! In the night. Especially
in the summer. Night like this. And I guess uh...you do too.
Nothing wrong. We're stoic New Yorkers. A dying breed. Out
alone. Late at night. Having a drink or two. Then a little walk.
And now a chit-chat on a corner. Nothing wrong with that. No
laws broken. No sir. No. None.

Who...uh... I just left that bar over there. That one on the
corner. And I was head up enjoying this lovely night. Just walking
alone, minding my own, and then down and out I went. And you...
saved me. Literally. Thank you. But on my own behalf, I must

75

say I did not drink too much in that bar. I'm not some drunk or something. Maybe one or two, but not much more. No! I'm certainly no lush. Adventurous—yes! But a boozer—no! And even if I did, I can hold my liquor, fella. There's Russian in my family. Anyway...well...so here I am chatting away like we're old war buddies. And I really don't even know you, do I! Do I? Anyway, maybe I...uh, did have a little too much to drink, or my blood sugar is off or something, but I am still a little light headed and floaty, *(joking)* and I'd hate to visit ole Mr. Curb again. And...since you are standing right here. Perhaps...if it's not asking too much... Maybe you'd be so kind...to help me over to my apartment. I live right over there. That building. So close. And you were so strong...in helping me. And I do live so close...literally! I would be so obliging to you. Really...my deepest gratitude. If you could just help me...back to my room. Please, I know it's asking a lot... since...we don't even know each other. But we fellow New Yorkers, right? And I am... so dizzy. Please, may we continue our little chat up at my place. Thank you again, for saving me from the curb. My fellow New Yorker. And...it's right over here. Uh... My name is...Mary-Anne.

EVA

Eva - 20's-30's - Liberty Island

It is a few days after the great Apocalypse and most of the world
has been destroyed. Eva's decided to take her kids over to
Liberty Island for a day trip. While there, she meets another
woman and they strike up a friendship.

EVA: *(Optimistic, and guileless)* Day after the Apocalypse, I was
sittin' around. Stunned. Like everybody. You too? Yeah.
Wasted. But... I just couldn't...sit there anymore. Y'know what
I mean? In that rubble. I don't know. So I grabbed my kids and
we started off down to Battery Park, like on a whim or somethin'.
Walked, of course. Nothin's workin' anymore. We hadda walk.
We live...lived way up on West seventy-third, right off what was
once the park. Walked downtown. Unbelievable, the chaos.
Nothing's left.

Anyway, when we got down to the ferry, I was shocked. I
mean, cause it was running. The ferry. Something was still
working. Nothin' else is. It's like they knew y'know. That
people'd need to come out here to look—see the whole thing.
Y'know what I mean? And that ride over, lady, let me tell ya.
See'n the city—what's left of it—for the first time. I mean,
staggering. Yeah. Overwhelming! But you could see forever.
Clean, clear through. Incredible. The view. *(looking out)*
S'breathtaking, isn't it?

My kids, Alex and Andrea, they were havin' a ball on the
boat. Y'know kids—s'a whole new playground for them.

(calling off) "Alex! Leave Andrea alone. *Alone! Don't
hit!* Honey, don't let him hit you. No. Play nice, both of you.
And keep away from the water! Don't touch any of that stuff
floating in... *(back to friend, smiles)* Kids. Anyway... So, we've
been comin' out here just about every day. Somethin' ta do,
y'know?

They feed us. And s'like more and more people keep
comin' each day. Like pilgrimages.

We try ta get here before the sun comes up. It's somethin'
to see it comin up... *(looking)* So open out here. Magic.
Spectacular in a crazy way, isn't it? Kids love it too. S'hypnotic.

EVA

(then softly) Why you think it happened? Things weren't that bad.
Were they? I didn't... I don't know. I didn't think... *(then)* I
thought it was a bomb. Didn't you? Everyone did I guess. We'd
just finished breakfast. Kids were gettin' ready for school. And
then it got dark. Remember? Night in day. And then that light.
That eerie, pink light. Then the smell, I'll never forget it. And the
blue. The blue. The beautiful, beautiful blue. I can still see it,
can't you? That blue? It was everywhere, And then...I grabbed the
kids. We got under the table. Held on. The kids screamin'.
Everyone was, I guess. Screams. Until the noise. Remember.
Deafening. My ears. *(she puts her hands to her ears)* I thought the
sky cracked. I thought the whole city exploded. I said to myself,
okay that's it. They did it. Dropped the bomb. Whoever. But it
wasn't no bomb, was it? No. No.

And after... *(fading)* After—after—after—after—after.
Well...

You see the signs goin' up? Funny, huh? "Future home of
the New World Deli." "New World Dry Cleaners." New World
this. New World that. Back to business soon. Everything'll be
back before you know it. Life goes on. But this time *better*. I
believe that. I do. Better.

There's a reason for everything. And it's gonna be better
this time. New and improved! Second chance. Yeah! The new go-
round. "New World." I like the sound of it. Don't you? "New
World." Yeah! Kind of Hollywoodish with just a bit of Bethlehem
thrown in. Ha, well yabba-yabba-yabba. We gotta get goin'. Sun's
comin' up.

(calling off) Andrea, come on. Alex, hurry up.

(back to friend) Hey, you wanna come with us. Come on.
We go way up to the torch. Up there you can see till the end of the
earth. Nothin' blocks the view anymore. Up there there's nothin'
but high hopes and possibilities.

Come on. Come with us. It'll make you feel better, you'll
see. C'mon. No, don't look back. Look up. C'mon. Good. I
don't know about you, but me, I love to watch the sun come up.
It's...so wonderful.

BETH

Beth - Any age - A street
Beth is a timid, tense, terrified lady. Everything and everyone
in the city scares her. In this monologue she describes her
nightly journey coming home from the subway.

BETH: *(She's prim and proper, speaks quickly and is slightly
hysterical.)*
>They're like little black creatures
>>Who hide in the night.
>
>Just waiting in doorways,
>>All ready to leap.
>
>But I try to get home from the subway alive.
>It' a war on the streets to survive.
>Each night.
>Coming home.
>All my jewelry is hidden.
>My money is stashed.
>I walk tall.
>Act brave.
>Move fast. Fast!
>Street lights are friends.
>>They're pools of safety.
>
>My mace is clutched,
>>>prepared,
>>>>and ready.
>
>To throw at those rapists,
>>Who try and attack me.
>
>As I run with my hands in the air—Help!
>>to the phone booths.
>
>Which are useless
>>>to dial 911.
>
>'Cause they've broken the phones.
>>And stolen the coins.
>
>Then hope that you'll try,
>So they can lock you inside.

BETH

And probably set it on fire. Oh, Lord!
Rooftops are covered
    with snipers with guns.
Muggers are mugging everyone
    that I pass as my heels are clicking away.
And the mice go scampering by.
        As I'm
    running, praying,
    thinking of home.
    Dreaming of safety,
        just being alone.
Off of these mean streets,
        with all that I own.
        So huddled and out of harms's way.
Where I've
    TV and comfort,
    And bars on my windows.
    Burglar alarms that will warn and protect me.
    Medeco locks,
    and neighbors who know,
    that if I scream in the night,
        it's a plea.
    A call for them,
        from me.
    And they always come running,
        always,
            Thank God!
But enough.
No more.
I'm home.
My breathing is back.
I have arrived.
My building's entrance is a shrine.
Bringing tears to my eyes.
    Like a Heaven's gate opening for me.

BETH

Slowly I enter the inter-comed,
       securitied,
       double-latched front doors.
Checking mirrors in hallways,
       to see I'm not followed.
I take out my key when I get to my door...
       but Lord! Look, it's slightly ajar.
Lights on,
       inside.
Who?! What?! How?!
There's a hand on my shoulder.
       Jesus... What do I think?
              I turn around slowly... And...
It's... the super, the super! Who says,
"Hi ma'am. Sorry. I still fixing you sink."
"Oh, my sink!" I say. "My sink, of course!"
I breathe,
       collapse,
           and fall into a chair.
He looks at me and says, "You ok? You want, I get outta
       here."
"Oh no no no no. Stay. Please. Stay. Really,
it's okay.   It's just been a very rough day.   You
understand." "Oh yes, ma'am," he says. And goes back to
fixing the sink.   While I make myself the biggest and
strongest stiff drink.
And begin to relax. Re-lax.
While watching him work.
Finally beginning to feel safe.
       Out of the war zone.
Snug here, in my home.
       Out of danger...
           Not frightened...
              At last!

CAROUSEL

Carousel - 20's-40's - A bar

Carousel's got the whole bar scene all figured out. There isn't a scene or an angle she hasn't played. Most importantly, Carousel must always be the star and be "featured."

CAROUSEL: *(big, hot and sassy)* Honey, *(finger snap)* I was "featured" last night. Uh-huh! I had these drop-dead earrings on, and a gown, uh! such a gown, that those dolls at the disco were *baleeched*. Girl, they were washed and put out ta dry. They knew, uh-huh, "Miss Thing" had finally arrived "sans entourage." I was fierce! I was hateful! And what ahm sayin' is, girl, I was "featured!" Um-hum. The trade woke up. I swear, I was more'n they could bare. I tell ya I got wet. Um-hum. Miss Diva-rama, *Qu-een* of the Downtown Scene. Where everybody there, judgin' by they "lack" a good taste, had purchased their drag a la Woolworth's; or somewhere equally cheesy. So next to them, I was a Hollywood starlet, night on the town, makin' the rounds. Lettin' the neon light my way; from club ta club—like Dorothy to Oz. A little "parlez-vous" with him— *(to him)* "Kunti Kinti! How ya doin' child?"—and then him. But always catchin' my light, y'all hear? Bein' seen from the brightest angle. *(an aside)* But never—never-ever lettin' ma drugs show! *(talking to him. a true coquette)* "Um-um. No-no. Daddy, s'just me! My personality! I'm *always* like this. Bubbly. Even in the morning. Call me. Come over. You'll see."

And then off I go sweedle-di-doe, to that next Mister Right in waiting.

Bars are for beauties girl. And I *took (finger snap)* this town by storm! "Miss Featurette." And those other dolls, they were ushers at my movie. Sisters on parade, y'all hear? Yeah!

'Twas a magical, magical night. I never wanted it to end. But thank you Miss Donna Summers, that last dance always comes. An' even after-hours clubs close. So I grabbed Chico, my Mister Once and Again, and said, "Take me home James. Don't let the sun catch me cryin'." And off we went in a fairyland puff. Poof!

An' when we got home, got into bed; Girl, once again, with my Mister Chico, I was "featured." *(a finger snap)*

SHIRL

Shirl - 30's-50's - Outside her bathroom door
Shirl's drunk again. Tonight's Mr. Wonderful has, for some
reason, locked himself in her bathroom. While anxiously
waiting for him to come out, Shirl shares her feelings about
love, loneliness, and the magic of movies.

SHIRL: *(to him in the bathroom—in a lonely, desperate, drunken
stupor. Water is running)* Baby?! You hear me?... Huh? Turn
down the water... Come on... C'mon out... Ahm waitin'.... *(to
herself)* You shouldn't keep a good woman waitin' too long. S'not
polite... *(to him)* I want some more wine... Vino!... Where'd you
put the vino? Huh?!... Shit! S'no more. *(to herself)* I already be
drunk an waitin'... *(to him)* You know I like you baby. Like you
alotalotalotalotalot. My fool. *(dramatically)* Take me to the
casbah. *(as Tallulah)* Daahling. Dahling. *(to herself)* My prince
from the bar. Well,...no ring, but the prince ain't bad. S'too soon...
but not too late. No. Maybe...tomorrow...tomorrow...at Tara.
Tara!! *(then, to him)* Rhett? Rhett, you in there? Scarlett's a
waitin'. Tara's fallen. Rhett, you hear me? You hear me?! TURN
DOWN THE GOD-DAMN WATER! *(as Scarlett)* Well... there
goes the South!... Come on, turn it down... Okay?... Okay, then
don't! See if I care... Who needs ya anyway! An now *I* want to be
alone! *(as Garbo)* I vaant to be alone. I *vaaant* to be alone. *(to
him)* Hey Rhett! I vant to be alone!... Shit! Are you comin' outta
there? TODAY?!... Huh?! Come on baby, ahm gettin' tired; and
lonely. Lonely baby... Sleepy... Too much vino. I want to sleep.
  (to him) Prince? Rhett?... Somebody? Is anybody in
there?... Is that really the water running?...or?... *(to herself—
dramatically)* Why ask for the moon, I already have the stars...
Yes... An they're in movies. Movies! Make believe movies...like
my men?... Waitin' for me... *(as Gloria Swanson)* Yes, I'm ready
for my close up, Mr. DeMille.
  (to him) Baby?... Mr. Magic?... Ya Maggies waitin',
Brick. Where are you? Huh? Maybe ahl see ya someday. When
ahm dreamin'. 'Cause I dream beautiful men... I do, I do! Don't
I?... Right?... Don't I?

83

ANNA

Anna - 30's-60's - A women's shelter
Anna, a homeless woman, has been broken by living out on the
streets for too long. She tries to make contact with another
woman in a shelter and warns her of the dangers of street life
and shelter living.

ANNA: *(A lonely woman in a shelter—trying to make a friend.)*
They keep secrets here.
Everyone does
But I'll be ya friend.
Tell ya what goes on.
We'll share things if you like, okay?
Like food and stuff.
Talk all night like kids.
Eat up dreams.
Be friends like at a slumber party.
Whatiya say? *(pause)*
Alright. That's okay.
I'll talk enough for the two of us anyway.
Hey... Hey, look at me. *(like a child)*
Look what I got.
Ta-da!
Don't tell anyone, but...
Anna's got booooooze.
Yeah.
You gotta stash it here.
Keep it hidden.
Fuck 'em. Fuck 'em!
They don't give a hoot.
Naaah.
An' this stuff loosens ya lip, y'know?
An' me—I loooooooves to talk.
All I need's someone to listen.
An' you be right there—next bed.

84

ANNA

Ya eyes lookin' to hear, right?
  Watch.
    Look at...
      Look at me.
        I'm a show
(dancing around) Yip-yap
               Yip-yap.
  All night.
  Non-stop.
  Lala-lala-lala.
Till I'm all talked out an' fall asleep.
Just watch.
  You don't have to say a thing.
You just...
     You sure?
       You sure you don't want a little
drink?
I can...
  Okay, okay.
  I'm no stranger to talkin' alone.
No ma'am.
  Not me.
     Rap. Rap. Rap.
What da hell.
  Sometimes you hit it here, and sometimes you don't.
Yeah... well.
You tired huh?
  I can see.
  Yeah. Me too.
  Real tired. Real tired.
(too loud) STREET SCENES ALL FUCKED UP!
(softly) Yeah... Right... Well...
Go ta sleep. Just turn around. Go ahead.

85

ANNA

Like I'm not here.

(softly) Forget about me.

(then) Be sure ta stuff ya stuff hon.

Cause they steal it.

Right from under ya.

Then whatya got?

Right!

(too loud) FUCK!

(softly) Go to sleep.

Sorry if I kept you up.

(whispering) I'll jus' talk softly...to myself.

Little bit more.

Till I'm talked out.

Then I'll sleep. *(takes a sip, smiles)*

Sleep good.

See you in the A. of M. babe.

They wake us real early, ya know?

(too loud) FUCK!

(softly) Well, sleep well, hon.

Y'know you're pretty girl. You are.

Nice.

Really nice...

Talking ta ya.

G'night.

Yeah... Um. Yeah.

THE WASH

Brenda - 20's-30's - A laundry in Memphis
Brenda's felt trapped with Moe and their kids for a long time.
Being their full-time maid and slave was not the kind of life
she'd planned on. She dreams of some day being free of them.

BRENDA: *(A tiny rundown laundrette in a small town, somewhere
in Memphis, late at night. Brenda, sitting on the bench, is lost in
thought, half watching the clothes spinning in the dryer. She begins
speaking slowly.)*
   Jus' sittin here
      on this ole bench. Needs a good paintin'.
   Thinkin'bout things.
      Lotsa things.
         While sippin ma Coke.
         Late night
            in this two bit cheapo laundrette.
Some town,
Some where,
    in Memphis.
Lord am I bored.
An' mama wuz you right.
    Sittin here
        watchin' them clothes go round.
Spinnin'.
      Round they go—over an over.
An when they through,
      s'back to Moe,
      an' the kids,
      in the trailer,
      parked in the parkin' lot,
        'bout two blocks from here.
Where them kids are right now tearin' up,
      an' makin' a mess, I guess.
While Moe—you jus' be sittin' there—as usual,

THE WASH

guzzlin' yo beer,
watchin' the T.V.,
thumbs a tappin'—impatient.
Waitin' for me
   to come back,
     an' pick up afta ya,
       like always.

You'll say,
   "Hey-hey, where you been girl? Huh? How come it took
ya so long? Ahl bet'cha been in some bar downtown, cattin' aroun',
lookin' for some."

Ahl say,
   "Moe... Shut up. Shut up! You're so damn dumb. An'
keep ya vile, dirty thoughts locked up in your dumb, empty head.
'Cause I don't wanna hear 'em anymore.

   An listen Moe, if I did want some, really, I wouldn't need
no laundry s'an excuse, ahd jus' do it. So you quit messin' with me,
hear? Fore I do do it. So don't tempt me, okay?"

   An Moe... Moe'll look a bit a shock, pause, an' then laugh
a lot. Like s'a big joke.

   "Ha ha, jus' kiddin'," he'll say.

   "Sure you wuz Moe. Sure you wuz. Like a pig's ass."
An' him finally catchin' ma drift, he'll say,

   "C'mon—c'mon, settle down. Come sit on ma lap. Relax.
C'mere girl. Warm it up fo' ya papa."

   "Warm it ya damn self Moe. An you ain't ma papa! Jus'
leave me A-lone. I'm tired and got a baaad headache. S'matta a
fact I got two. One's you, an one's them kids."

   An he'll start ta laugh again, thinkin' I wuz kiddin'. Then
the kids'll laugh. An everybody get hysterical, thinkin' s'a big joke.
   "Ha ha,
     Momma's foolin'.
     Momma's foolin'.
     Momma's jokin' around."

THE WASH

An them kids'll roll over an bust a gut laughin'. An' drunk Moe'll give me a big wink.

An me, ahl jus' stand there, ma hands on ma hips, dumbfounded in disbelief, that nobody gets that I meant it. Exactly what I said, that I'd rather live alone in the cold a Siberia, or nursin' the poor crippled lepers of Africa, than stay stuck with them in this mouse trap trailer of a home. Unable to breathe anymore, or think ma thoughts. Always boxed in and closed. Why...s'no different than them clothes jammed together in that dryer—spinning tight into that go-round cycle, over an over, over an over, every-day.

Seems like them clothes an me got a great deal in common. Only difference is I can free them, but what about me?!

(She goes to the dryer, and throws open the door)
"Come on out you clothes, ready or not, I am...the LAUNDRY LIBERATOR come to your rescue! Ya had enough hot air for one night. Out! Everyone!" *(puts her hand in to grab clothes)*

"Well, well, right here on top, it's Moe's jeans. Yes, ya been washed, and now ya clean. Get the hell outta ma life!" *(She starts frantically throwing clothes out of the machine)*

"Panties, towels, shirts, socks, everybody out. Everybody's liberated! Right now! Independence Day in the laundry room. Welcome to the world a the livin'. Come on out! I'm breakin' the cycle tonight. Not goin' roun' no more. Wet or dry—you free!

An' looky-looky, why here's Moe's favorite button down shirt. *(she rips it.)* Ooops! I ripped ya. Sorry Moe, the machine musta done it. An... look, here's your nice under shorts *(she rips it.)* Damn! There's a little tear. *(she rips it again.)* An' there's another. Now ya can pee from two places Moe!"

(wildly, she continues throwing clothes out, all over, in total abandon.) "All you clothes, c'mon! Come on! This way! Out! This way! OUT!

DAMN! DAMN! SHIT! SHIT! DAMN! What about... me! Whenz it my turn? When can I go free! I gotta go back! I have ta...I...or...or...do I? Do I have to do anything?!

89

THE WASH

Listen...Listen ta me Moe! Listen good! You tell them kids, that their momma closed shop tonight! Suddenly! The laundry lady left...for points unknown. *Unknown*, Moe!

The cleanin' lady...cleaned up! An took off...for anywhere. Anywhere Moe!... Where there's breathin' space. An' people don't laugh at'cha when ya ain't kiddin'.

An Moe...don'cha dare miss me. Don't. 'Cause I won't miss you.

An tell them kids, their momma left with nothin' but the clothes on her back. Tell them kids that. That momma went off...somewhere...lookin' for somethin' better. An when they're old enough, they'd be smart ta do the same. An'... Don't you miss me Moe. Come to the laundry and get'chor clothes. 'Cause from now on ya better take care a things ya own...or they'll disappear.

(Slowly she walks over the pile of clothes on the floor towards the door. She turns back, looks around, smiles)

"S'long laundry.

S'long clothes.

See ya.

Bye...

Thanks.

(she leaves)

90

ANGELA

Angela - 20's-40's - A bar
Angela is an adept game player in the bar scene. She has mastered the art of being a turn-on and a tease. Sometimes coy, always cunning, she usually gets her man exactly where she wants him.

ANGELA: *(like a seductive spider in a web.)*
> And zoom zoom zoom, I met a guy.
> And zoom zoom zoom, we go out a while, and he pops the question.
> A triple zoom later, we're married and then divorced.
Okay, so I'm back on the road again, looking for Mr. Right, or even Mr. Wrong, if he can perfect himself. When in walks "The Man." I'm saying, *"The Man"* I have always dreamt about. The eyes, the nose, the walk, the savoir—fairest creature in all maledom.
> And he give me such a look of beckoning and "come and get it," that my heart buckles, and my knees collapse. And I am unable to lift myself off the bar stool.
> So he meanders downstream to my locale, and I like "Lana Turner" him a look. And the fun begins.
> Let me tell you, this man puts an indent on the word, "Charm." He goes way beyond smooth.
> And we're doing a "ring-a-rosey" of get know ya's, when he whispers, *(whisper)* "Let's go back to my place and fool around." At which point, his hands begin to touch and sample, and paw me in bits.
> As true coquette, I say, "Please don't," and giggle, "I'm not that kina' girl."
> "Aw, c'mon," he says, and continues groping, en masse.
> "Don't!" I said. "I don't like it! And if you don't stop, I will kick you in the balls so hard that your shit will turn blue and your eyes will pop out of your head!"
> His eyes took on a somewhat terrified glaze, and he squirmed, "Are you serious?"

ANGELA

"Try me!" I smiled like a razor.

Slowly he began to disengage his "tentacles" as our eyes never lost contact.

"I am a lady," I said softly. "You, on the other hand, are vermin and scum."

I took my drink and *threw* it in his face. "Don't you ever come near me again, Mister!"

And dripping wet, he crawled away.

I sighed, and then got back up on my bar stool, and ordered another drink.

And zoom zoom zoom, I looked around again.

And zoom zoom zoom, couldn't wait to play.

LISA

Lisa - 20's-30's - Backstage at a theatre

Lisa's dream was to be a great actress. After getting a leading role in a show and tremendous encouragement during rehearsals it looked like she was on her way to becoming a star. But on opening night, just a few minutes before she's to go on, a disaster occurs. She discovers that her "character" has deserted her.

LISA: *(a young ingenue)*
>I am frozen on this chair
>>in my costume.
>
>The lines from the script
>>flood my brain.
>
>But...but my character's gone.
>Where?
>She left with my breath.
>I'm a shell in a frame.—Who am I?
>>And what is my name?
>
>Oh no! Can't be!
>>Five minutes,
>>Five minutes,
>>>till curtain.
>
>Who's this lady I see in the mirror,
>in that wig,
>>and the make-up,
>>>and now tears.
>
>So frightened,
>Such fear.
>I must get out of here,
>>And run to the director and cast.
>
>I'll plead.
>I'll try to explain.
>>Just...delete my name.
>>Uh...pull it from the playbill.

LISA

Say...
>Say...due to death,
>>She came and went.

Her character fled,
>And now she's dead. And...

Four minutes,
Four minutes till curtain. No!
Calm down.
Try to breathe.
Where is my breathe?!
Gone—with my character, I guess.
What is an actress without her character?
And I was so radiant in rehearsal.
The director,
>All of the cast,
>>Said, "Some day—Broadway!"

But I had my character then.
And she moved me with such grace.
We had a life—she and I—sparkling.
Each moment was a new thrill on the stage.
An adventure.
"Where are we going? Take me with you."
Away from this town,
>Everything new.

A "big" life.
So unlike mine,
>Confined to such small places.

My character was a friend who fed me.
But she's gone.
And I'm here alone in a dressing room,
>On a chair—waiting...

For my public execution out there.
Three minutes.
Three minutes...till death.

LISA

The audience wants magic.
The theater is coming to a hush.
Make-up—retouched.
The wig—just one more brush.
It's too late—to run.
Who I am will have to do.
Since my character's gone,
And there is no one else,
Tonight I'll try something new.
I'll say the words as *I* feel them,
With my own sense of power and dignity.
Yes, since my charcter's gone,
The only thing left,
Is that I play my role as me. Me!
That's to be my little secret,
As I walk through the backstage dark into the light.
My character may be gone,
But the play must go on.
And this will be *my* opening night!
One minute...
One minute till magic.
And my dawns early light on the stage.
My character's still gone,
So long, sweet friend.
This show—tonight's for you.

VELVET

Velvet - 30's-50's - A bar

Usually, Velvet thinks of herself as a no-nonsense business woman. But one night she met a very exciting man who showed her a whole new side of herself.

VELVET: *(She is standing at the bar holding a half-empty glass of white wine. She is around forty years old, conservatively dressed, mildly attractive, slightly prim and proper.)* Licking my lips, like this. *(she does)* Then wetting them down with my finger. *(she does)* Smiling that smile you do when you want something. Like this. *(she shyly smiles)* And letting him know. And he did, oh yes. Letting him know...and he did.

It was right here. This very spot. Here. Finishing my drink. Watching him. Saying yes with my eyes. Yet, still trying to be a lady. But when you want something, and it's been a long day, work was hard, the boss on top of you every minute pushing towards a deadline. There's too much pressure. Too much! So I came here to the bar for a drink. And now...then wanting someone to...rub my back. *(to an imaginary him)* "Please... Yes. Go ahead. Any way you want to. Go ahead. *(a smile)* Be creative. Yes. Yes! Find my weak spot."

So, he walked over. Said hello. We talked, and he started to play with my hand. Said my skin was soft. And then he called me "Velvet." I took the straw from my drink, put it in my mouth, bit down, and smiled. He smiled back. The red neon sign outside the window was going on and off, on and off, on and off.

I bit down on the straw even more. My mind was floating in the gutter, and he knew it. He knew it.

He asked me if I wanted another drink. I said, "I don't need it." And then I blushed and we both laughed.

Finally, I said, "Well?" And he he said "Yeah." And I said, "Okay."

He had this white car. Long and white with the top down. It was a warm night. Very warm. We got in and drove. Very fast.

VELVET

My arm, hanging out the window. My hand, cupping the wind. I watched him, and let my knee touch his...slightly. He was...the most handsome black man I had ever seen! Ever! A prince. A king!

We got to my hotel, walked in, went to the elevator. Everything in me was barely holding on. I didn't care what anybody thought. I...couldn't wait. In the elevator...I was crumbling!

"Nice hotel," he said.

(sensual whisper) "I want you in my bed," I said.

The elevator stopped. We go off, made it to the room. The key—it opened, and in. And inside I lost all sense of anything—anything civilized. And he carried me to the bed, took off his shirt, stood there. I clutched the pillow, and watched, as he slowly took off his pants. My dress flew to the chair! He played with my toes. Licked...each...one. I couldn't wait. I...

Some men... Some men know. They just know how to make love to a woman. How to make her happy, excite, and... satisfy completely. COM-PLETELY! And he was that kind of man. He knew. Oh yes, he knew! The man I met that night was a king. And I, gratefully, was no longer a lady. I allowed myself to be...undignified. And we ran every red light. I was drained and filled at the same time! And the bed was wet! Soaking!

And all through it he kept saying, *(softly)* "Nice. Nice Velvet. Nice." As the day disappeared. And my job didn't matter. And the pressure, the pressure...was released. *(a long exhale)* Oooooohhh! Just...oh. When there's nothing else you can say to describe. When words fail—oh!

Later, when I looked up at him, I said, "Must you go?" He was dressing, he smiled, kissed me on the cheek, and said "Yes."

"Wait," I said. I took three crisp fifty dollar bills from my bag. "Here. Is that right?"

He smiled.

I said, "Another night soon?"

"Nice Velvet," he said. "When you're ready and want me—

VELVET

You know where. You know when.

    (smiling) So...here I am. And there he is...again.

    Like deja-vu.

    But truly... Yes... It has been...another rough, rough day at the office.

VERNICE

Vernice - 20's-40's - A dressing room in a strip joint
Vernice, a stripper, loves being a woman who can arouse men.
A customer from the club where she works has come back to
her dressing room to ask for a date.

VERNICE: *(with a heightened sensuality—to an imaginary man)*
You gotta shake your booty with extravaganza in the South.
The "what's behind that?"
Then looky-looky, gets 'em crazy in those clubs.
But Mister, *my* act is one of class and vision.
I am the female nymph ascending.
My act is hot with declare.
But then, "oh-no-no," not too much.
I stay a lady—always Mister.
I have satin and feathers with dim pastel lighting.
A *long* stretched leg—all naked and white.
And I move on the stage like the sirens of the forties.
There's mystery.
There's vamp.
There's heat incandescent.
I am a *woman*, and I love this attention.
I am a *woman*, and I need this escape.
The men arouse and want me—begging me for favors.
I kiss through a smile that lifts them from their seats.
A little more!
A little more!
But never too much sir.
You'll think you've seen it all. But it's just an illusion.
It all looks good though. The package is finely wrapped.
Then I'm exposed throughout the show.
And like a woman—
I'm a riddle.
   And a paradox.
    And a puzzle.

VERNICE

Can't you see?
Don't you get it?
Let me tell you—
I'm a man.
       In a woman.
              In a show.
But as far as you're concerned,
I perform
In an act
On the stage.
I give you what you want.
What you've come for.
What you need!
What's the difference?
It's all make believe, anyway. (Isn't it?)
So, enjoy what I have to offer.
Believe me—it's the best of me that you're getting.
We both love the mystique of the lady.
       Of the feminine.
       Of woman.
Look at me—all form and grace.
Now, go back, and sit in your seat.
And please, Mister—Enjoy the show.

ANGEL

Angel - 20's-40's - A piano bar
Feeling stuck in a cold water flat in New Jersey with a junkie husband, Angel always dreamt of escaping to New York to become a famous singer. Here she recalls the night she took the risk and followed her dream.

ANGEL: *(A Latin lady with a lot of gusto)*
> He loved ta call me "Angel."
> Angel, yeah.
> Angel this,
> An' Angel that.
> "Angel c'mere!"
> "Angel, you heard me, get me a fuckin' beer!!"
Well, his little "Angel" wanted outta there.
'Cause what was heaven for him—
> Was hell fa me.
An' more than anything, I needed ta be free.
> So one mornin'
> 'Fore the crack a dawn,
> He's still asleep,
> An' I am packed up an gone.
>> Just-like-that.
>>> Shit, yeah!
> S'like playin' cards, y'know?
> 'Cept ya get jus' one hand.
> One shot.
> That's it—ya life.
An' me, I didn't wanna spend mine in Jersey,
>> some junkie's wife.
(angry; to him) Not me! Not me baby!
(the big dream) I got NBC-TV-peacock-Technicolor dreams.
> An' more than anything,
>> anything,
>>> I had a dream ta sing.

ANGEL

                                    Yeah, sing!
        In a cabaret,
                Or on Broadway.
                        Don't matter.
        Jus' give me openin' nights at Sardi's.
        Fancy clothes,
                Paparazzi an' parties.
Barbara Walters interviews.
My pictures in the papers,
        My name in the news.
                Fame! Shit! YEAH!
        An' so I left him that night.
                (cutesy; to him) "Bye-bye."
        Got on a Greyhound.
        Took the five a.m. Purgatory Express
        Got me a seat, looked out,
                an' waved good-bye ta nobody.
        (to him) You hear me baby, NOBODY. NO ONE!
        But didn't matter,
                I kept wavin' anyway.
                        An' wavin'
                        An' wavin'
                                AN' WAVIN'! SON OF A
BITCH!
        I don't know why,
                but all of a sudden on that bus, I started ta cry.
        Because I felt...
                like somebody had died.
        An' as that bus drove from the darkness ta the light,
        Angel crossed over to the other side.
        So what ahm sayin', what ahm sayin' is,
                if heaven's here,
                        an' hell is on earth,
        (to him) Yeah, okay, I died on that bus, baby.

                            102

ANGEL

But there was also a birth.
An' now, now I sing here
                every single night.
       Any song *I* want!
       Any song *I* need!
       Any song *I* like!
Ballads,
       or blues, I don't care. Don't matter.
S'just Mister Piano Man an' me.
       Singin' some songs,
             but finally famous,
                    like I've always wanted ta be.
                    An' now your little Angel baby
                    is flyin' high. Look—can't you see?
                    Angel now is on her own
                        An' I'm finally,
                              finally,
                                    free!

KATHY

Kathy - Any age - Anywhere
Night time was special for Kathy because she knew she'd always
see her father. He would tuck her into bed, give her a good-
night kiss, and promise to see her later in her dreams.

KATHY: *(a young girl—a painful memory)*
    And my Daddy said,
    When you put your head on the pillow
        and go to sleep,
    You go to the Feather Ball.
    And if I did...
        If I did,
            He'd see me there.
    And I listened to my Daddy,
        because he knew.
    Yes, he was so smart.
        And I was just a little girl.
    But I believed in him.
    And so I'd close my eyes,
        And I'd see it,
            Just like he said.
    Oh, it was so beautiful.
    It was the most beautiful place I had ever been.
        All dreamlike,
            and magical,
                and make believe.
    But best of all,
        I knew that my Daddy was coming soon.
    And so I would go to sleep,
        like a good little girl,
            waiting for him.
    As the feathers fell,
        and the music played,
            and I was ready to dance.

KATHY

My day was over.
And Night Time was here.
And I was in bed,
    And at the Feather Ball,
        Dreaming....and waiting.

STELLA

Stella - 30's-40's - A pick-up bar
When Stella makes love to a man her mind drifts off to places
far away. Her fantasies have little to do with the man she's
actually with. This is the story of one of her sexual encounters.

STELLA: *(sensuously)* I slipped up to him at the bar, and
whispered, "Are you Sergeant Pepper, baby?" He smiled, just like
little boy lost. And my eyes shot out, "Come to momma, come to
momma!"

His smile broadened, and his eyes said, "Let's party baby!"

And as he spoke, I watched his eyes, and began playing in
a dream of going off to Mozambique, lying naked with this handsome stranger in a lush green field, making crazy burning hot love
under a tropical storm.

"Oooh. It's awful noisy here," I sighed, to my boy in the
bar. "Why don't we go back to my place, and check out some
etchings, ya know."

So me and my Ferdinand the Bull took a right to heaven,
and climbed through the night sky in his white charger, finally
landing at "Mi Casa of Dreams."

"Can I getcha a drink or somethin'?" I moaned.

From his ever-broadening smile, I believe I heard him
gurgle a "yes." So I did, ya know. And shortly thereafter, we got
cozy. Real cozy. Then we comfied into each others private
"styles." And he touched me. And kissed me. And slurped all
over me; as I sailed on a big boat...to Bora Bora. Alone, but soon
meeting another handsome stranger. And we drank pink champagne
and Mimosas, threw our glasses out into the ocean, caught a sunset,
and made passionate, exotic love, and laughed ourselves out to sea.

"God, you're good!" I *lied* to baby boy blue. "Can you
please stay over tonight?" His smile broadened to beyond his ears,
as he howled, "Forever, baby!"

So me and my "Forever Baby!", cood, and held, and
stroked, and caressed, as I disappeared to Siam, to become the

Kings' new concubine. And I most joyfully serviced my powerful majesty's every whim. Yes! And he worshipped me totally, and made me his Royal Queen. And the skies opened, and all the angels sang, as we made love night and day for all eternity.

When I opened my eyes, Ferdy was staring at me so dreamily.

"Where were you?" he cood.

"Heaven," I sighed.

"Was it as good for you as it was for me?"

"Good?! Baby, it was beyond good. I went to places...you only dream about."

"You are something else," he whispered.

"Yeah," I smiled.

HANNAH

Hannah - 20's-40's - A bar
All her life Hannah has always been the polite, sweet little girl.
With men she always feigns complete interest in their every
word, and makes sure to always have a loving smile pasted on
her face.

HANNAH: *(In the bar. He is talking. She is inside herself.)*
Shhhhh! Shhhhh! Please. Please stop talking....and look at me.
Look at me for just one moment. I'm here! Don't you see me?
Don't you see me? I can't smile much more. It's starting to hurt.
I'm trying so hard to look...interested. Like...I care. Like...I want
to be here with you in this dirty—smokey, hell hole bar. My eyes
are burning. Can't you see? Or...are you so preoccupied with your
own words... words...that fly me away to the beach that day.
Alone! I'm lost. "Daddy! I'm lost! There's sand in my mouth.
I'm burning! Where are you? I'm scared! Daddy! The ocean is so
big. The sun...burns! I'm lost. It frightens me"... to *(back in the
bar)* be sitting next to you on this bar stool...pretending. Making
believe we're together. We're not.

Do you think...I'm pretty?

I'll sit here politely...yes...like a good little girl. Third
row...fourth seat...hands clasped in front of me. They all know...
every boy and girl...that I am the best. The best little girl in the
class. And I am. I am...so good. So good *(back to the bar)* that
you don't even see me. So good...that...I'm disappearing. And
soon my pretty dress and lovely hair will float softly to the floor.
And you won't even notice. Will you? Will you?! Will you!! No.
You'll just turn to the lady next to you... and begin again. Telling
her how wonderful you are. And she'll smile too. And she'll
pretend to listen, and try to breathe, and hold herself together so that
she won't disappear. We want to make you happy.

More than life...more than who I am... I'll sit here with
you tonight, in this noisy, smoke filled, hell hole bar, hoping
you'll... admire me...and...make me happy. See my smile. See my
smile! It is...just for you...baby!

ROSE

Rose - Any age - A bar
Rose has been dumped on by men all her life. But last night
something changed and she finally defended herself.

ROSE: *(with joyful revenge)* When I said "no" to him, it was like
saying "no" to all the garbage in my life!

I said, "I've been around this Monopoly board too many
times mister, and you can just go south, 'cause I am passing 'Go'
this time!"

He stood there, dumbfounded, and said, "What's wrong?"

I said, "Guys like you always get what'cha want, don'cha?
Well, from me, it's not here!, not now!, not ever again!

Guys like you have been burning my tail for too long, and
then leaving me naught. Well I have decided I'm a lot more than
naught! A lot more! So you just better get outta my way!"

"What I do wrong?" he whined.

"YOU BREATHE!" I said. "I'm gonna find me a good
man. A man who knows how to treat a Lady. And I *am* a Lady,
in case you haven't been looking! I'm more than just a Lady, I'm
a grown woman. And any guy that gets me, gets the best!

So... I know you think you're El Primo Stud around this
dump. Well, you better start struttin' your stuff, Mister Cocksure,
'cause you're about to see a Lady take an exit!"

LULU

Lulu - 30's-40's - At her close friend's apartment
Desperately looking for a man, Lulu thought she finally found
one. But as so many times before, Mr. Right is another dud.
And once again, Lulu is crushed.

LULU: *(agitated)* Don't repeat my words! Don't repeat 'em! I
know what I said. I know *exactly* what I said. I was there,
remember?! But that was then, and this is now. And Prince
Charming is history. 'Cause as far as I'm concerned, he was just a
lovely dream. A visit. A fantasy...that ended. I woke up. Another
morning. That's it!

It's just that... Sometimes...sometimes...with the night, and
the music...and in the dark, words are spoken, softly, or whispered.
And in the context of that moment—there's magic. It's everything.
It seems like... Yes! Yes! He's it. *This* is the man. Hello! And
it's love. Love, that fleeting emotion that puts a spell on us, and
makes us all go nuts!

And so we think, in the long term scheme of things, that...
well, maybe...who knows?! Maybe... Maybe...he's it. He's...the
one. The one!

But. And it's a big but, reality sneaks in sometimes, and
you realize...

> He's too short,
> he's too tall,
> wrong sign,
> funny body.

Any one of a million things that sheds light on the fact that he's...not
the man. Sorry. And all the romance and blah-blah-blah in the
world won't make it right. All of the wishes, and FTD flowers, and
candy can't make him the person that I want to spend the rest of my
natural life with; pouring out babies for, and wearing his name till
death does us both into the grave. No.

Look, I know. I know I've been telling you how hard I've
been looking. Under every rock. And I'll continue to look, believe

me. Even if my search takes me to the boondocks. Or somewhere, some jungle retreat where my personal Tarzan, in a loin cloth, sits waiting. 'Cause with the right turn of events, I can be Jane for anyone. You know that. No sacrifice too great.

But this guy—this man from the other night was neither Tarzan nor Prince. Believe me. And that's that! And it's okay. It is. I'm alright. Look, do I not look like I'm okay? Huh? I'm fine. I'm fine! You cut your losses, and what will be will be. And life goes on in the singles bars, right? I mean it's one down, one more to go. Alright?

So you're wondering, "What happened? What brought this on?" I'll tell you. So...when he called this morning, oh, I was so lovey dovey. Honey this and honey that. Well, it came out on the phone, that the son of a bitch told me he was married. And has four kids, and lives upstate somewhere.

So...on the phone, I didn't feel I had too much to say; other than, "Oh... Oh... Well, best of luck... Thanks for dinner..." And I believe I even threw in, "regards to your wife."

So that's it. Why it's over. He's married. Ain't that a bitch?! And with a family of twelve years, four kids, upstate. And so I don't have to much else to say other than, boy, can I ever pick 'em. That rat bastard is married!... And not to me. No. Boy oh boy. Boy...oh boy.